Conversation

Thinking

About

Talking

Speech is civilization itself.
—Thomas Mann

Bill Hutman & Thomas O'Dwyer

Contents

Introduction

He has occasional flashes of silence that
make his conversation perfectly delightful.
　　　　　　　　　　—Sydney Smith

Xenophon. Ever heard of him? One of us hadn't and thought, *Oh, yes, he must be talking about the guy who came up with the idea of xenophobia, the fear of foreigners.* Luckily, he kept that comment to himself. Not that either of us would have given the other a hard time for saying something stupid. Just that it might have taken us off-topic, and that would have been a real shame.

Now don't ask us exactly what the topic was—as we don't remember that either. But we are sure it was a good one. By that time in the evening (or even sometimes in the afternoon), the topics were always interesting. The kind that got you shouting or just pensive, certainly engaged and thoughtful. Depending on the amount of alcohol consumed and the subject, things would get proportionally warm. Never to the point of physical confrontation, of course, but temptingly close.

Many times, friends have just thrown up their hands and walked out on us. "What the hell are you guys shouting about?" Or more likely, "You have no idea what you're talking about. You've got your heads up your ass." We could get riled on almost any topic, not just politics and religion. The odd exception is sports. Never, probably because we each defined football differently, being European and American, respectively—no hometown allegiances to defend.

We were both journalists at one time and continue to work in a profession, which we will explain later, where geopolitical developments are central. So we always followed the big stories of the day. In some instances, we even had knowledge and insight into issues not available to the general public, not to mention strong opinions about breaking news topics. Yet we share a sense that the hot topics of the day, whatever they may be, are just that, of the day and so there is no reason to get too angry over them.

Hah! How smug that previous paragraph looks now—"knowledge and insight into those issues not available to the general public" indeed. Just after we finished the draft of this book, our verbal indulgences over lunch got slapped sideways with the rest of the world. Conversation in the time of corona became more problematic than *Love in the Time of Cholera* for the protagonists of Gabriel García Márquez's novel. One of us (let's not say who) had barely time to start an argument along the lines of "this coronavirus thing is such a load of crap and tabloid hype" before being swept into a pandemic world of real isolation and virtual conversation. Had *The Matrix* been prophetic? A dot of protein that could be seen only with an electron microscope had incarcerated the advanced civilization of an entire planet. Want to chat about that (at a fixed distance) over a glass of Chardonnay?

In various sections of this book, we debate the impact of the digital world on conversation. We mostly reject the gloomy theory that smartphones are killing convivial chatter. It is too soon to pontificate here about the long-term social ramifications of the pandemic—your chattering heads online and in the media are taking care of that. There will be much to analyze as the data accumulates about the consequences for the art of conversation. But there are some encouraging small signs. Everybody has noted the uncomfortable drawbacks of video meetings—the shifty eyes, the absence of subtle body signals, the inclination to perform rather than relate. A previous decline in phone-calling in favor of texting and emailing reversed itself. The smartphone became just a phone again, and conversations on it became longer and more engaged.

We have become sharply aware that the real topics of interest to all of us are not the hot ones of the news day after all—does anyone want another exchange of half-baked and ever-changing information on COVID-19? (*The New York Times* ran a feature on how to start a conversation about something other than the virus. It even included a list of suggested opening sentences). Real topics are the opposite of hot. They touch on the enduring issues that we face as individuals and societies. Do we dare call them "bigger" and "more important" issues? Of course not, but before we begin to explain what we mean, let's get back to the topic we started with.

In those receding days of social conviviality, we were sitting in the Family Nest restaurant in the Strovolos neighborhood of Nicosia, Cyprus. Somehow (perhaps Greek food and Greek wine lead to Greek topics) we discussed how Xenophon today is known to classicists and philosophy lovers as a Greek philosopher-general. But he was at heart just a regular guy. Okay, maybe not that regular—he had many more responsibilities. But he also had regular habits, good and bad. Who doesn't like to go out for drinks with friends after work? Even in ancient Greece, they did. And when friends get together and start drinking, the conversation then as now gets loud. Most of the time, the talk is not about anything of importance, but sometimes it can get serious, and when you are a philosopher-general hanging out with your buddies, topics can get pretty heavy.

Xenophon was all for drinking and talking about life—as well as his philosophical theories or battle plans. He believed that a little alcohol gets the creative juices going so something interesting, even valuable, might emerge from the haze of an afternoon at the local *taverna* with your colleagues and friends. It could be a modified battle plan, a business idea for making millions, or an insight into one of the grand questions challenging humanity. But Xenophon wasn't stupid; he knew most of the hot air the gang spouted was boozy crap.

So he had a straightforward attitude. Philosophize, strategize, argue all you like over your wine carafes, but if any grand ideas float up, let's consider them soberly in the morning. If anything still sounds good, maybe we're on to something. Or maybe not. We aren't writing a book to encourage more drinking—that's not even required, but long lunches are. We'll explain later. We do think thoughts and ideas matter to everyone, not just philosophers and generals.

We are writing this book because conversation matters. Real conversations that don't require a PhD—or even an elementary school certificate. Yes, learning can matter, even the old-fashioned kind and the classics of literature, philosophy, history, art, and sciences.

Education is no more required for good conversation than alcohol, but we can still cite one of the classics without being branded elitist. *Alice's Adventures in Wonderland* is not so much a book of fantastic adventures as a book of conversations (and pictures). It's right there, in the first paragraph: "What is the use of a book," thought Alice, "without pictures or conversations?" Lewis Carroll and his illustrator John Tenniel delivered just that, a magical masterpiece of conversations and images. A reviewer of the time said it would "belong to all the generations to come until the language becomes obsolete." Six generations later, the language shows no sign of obsolescence, but the same cannot be said of conversations, if the great oracle at Google is correct. One million hits for "the death of conversation," it proclaims, listing a gloomy parade of studies and essays stretching back many years.

What commenters seem to decry about the death of conversation are not the essential dialogues that keep societies running—diplomatic and parliamentary debate, peace talks, economic or scientific discussions. The conversations they mourn are fuzzier: chats in cafés or beside metaphorical water coolers, animated arguments in bars about sports, discussions about books we pretend to read so we can meet and gossip, and the mind games of grifters, flirts and lovers.

The most common note of regret emerges at the sight of a couple sitting in a restaurant, their eyes fixed on their phones, tapping messages into some other digital world. Sad! They don't smile and talk to each other; they are not here but elsewhere, not together but alone. Yet has anything changed?

How short our memories are of the pre-device age when you could see "sad" couples in any café or restaurant, eating in stony silence. Had they nothing left to say? Or were they enjoying a cozy mutual silence that says, "We're here, together, and we're happy." And let's not exaggerate. Has anyone recently walked into a crowded café or bar and found it filled with silence? All those babbling people must be saying something, even if it's about their Facebook friends or their phone's battery life.

It's not the number of conversations we ought to be worrying about, but their nature. Most conversations are likely to be empty and meaningless—but not necessarily pointless. Some can be lost opportunities, and yes, some can be dangerous:

King: Who are you talking to?

Alice: It's a friend of mine—a Cheshire Cat: allow me to introduce it.

King: I don't like the look of it at all: however, it may kiss my hand if it likes.

Cat: I'd rather not.

King: Don't be impertinent. And don't look at me like that!

Alice: A cat may look at a king; I've read that in some book, but I don't remember where.

King: Well, it must be removed. [*To the Queen*] My dear! I wish you would have this cat removed!

Queen: Off with its head!

01 *What Are We Talking About?*

> *Don't knock the weather; nine-tenths of*
> *people couldn't start a conversation*
> *if it didn't change once in a while.*
> —Kin Hubbard

BRITISH WISDOM USED to advise that casual conversations with strangers should be limited to the weather and health. "Nice day"—"Yes, isn't it?"—"How are we today?"—"Can't complain." Goodbye to all that. As trolls throng out of cyberspace and into the real world, any trivial comment can set someone screaming for or against it. Nobody wants to start an early-morning argument about unsettled weather not being caused by climate change or about vaccinations spreading autism. As for banning discussions of religion and politics at the dinner table, that's a ship that long ago sailed and sank.

We define a conversation as an "oral exchange of sentiments, observations, opinions, or ideas." The *Oxford English Dictionary* mischievously cites a Samuel Johnson quote to illustrate that: "No, Sir; we had talk enough, but no conversation; there was nothing discussed." For Johnson, conversation was intellectual, and that's what made it different from small talk or banter. He expressed concern that any decline in proper political discourse would lead to social unrest. Those who have shared this concern for "good conversation" agree it is not small talk but has a higher purpose. Real conversation is both a means and an end, full of reason and emotion. It gives back; it makes you a better person.

The German philosopher Martin Buber made an interesting distinction between the two concepts of communication, which he called I–You and I–It. In typical turgid Germanic theology, he used his Ich–Du and Ich–Es to express the interpersonal nature of human existence, mainly through language. An I–You relationship between two beings is mutual, authentic, and respectful; the people communicate without needing to exchange either conviction or information. Buber's dense theology in his book *I and Thou* comes in when he uses his concept to explore communication between humanity and God. (What if there's no God? Don't ask, especially in German.) Yet even he could use plain words and everyday examples to illustrate real encounters. Two lovers, a man and his cat, a girl and a tree, two strangers on a train—all may have a dialogue, a conversation, or an exchange.

Buber's esoteric musing was prescient for the modern state of dialogue. I–You conversations recede, and I–It obsessions with smart devices are everywhere. Buber's I–You relationship develops in conversation only if we are open to it and make no demands. The other person (or cat) responds to our welcoming and willing gesture, and an encounter begins. The relationship lacks any structure and cannot be measured, but Buber stressed that it is real and will last as long as the individual wills it. Buber's I–It is the opposite of I–You:

instead of two beings engaging each other, they do not even meet. The "I" part defines its own idea of the other and treats it as an object. An I–It relationship is fake: it's with oneself; it is not a dialogue; it's a Trumpian tweet. It has the new skill of today's students—keeping eye contact with you, while texting elsewhere in cyberspace.

For Buber, everything was about being open to the "Other." You first think you get it; you get the meaning of that capital "Y." It's obvious, right? Wrong, you soon discover. That "You" is not just anyone (including God)—it should be everyone and more. Everything. It could be the guy who served you that espresso. Or the woman driving the taxi. Your busybody neighbor. Buber even uses a tree as an example and presents five separate relations "I" can have with "You," Tree. If you would open yourself to others, they can become Others. We can stop seeing these Others as objects—even a tree is no longer an It:

> If I face a human being as my Thou, and
> say the primary word I–Thou to him, he
> is not a thing among things, and does not
> consist of things. This human being is not
> He or She, bounded from every other He
> and She, a specific point in space and time
> within the net of the world; nor is he a
> nature to be experienced and described, a
> loose bundle of named qualities. But with

no neighbor and whole in himself, he is
Thou and fills the heavens.[1]

Buber's search for the universal "Other" led him not to
the heavens but to life around him on earth—life, or really
society, at its most basic level in people's connection with one
another. Buber discovered the spiritual in relationships. Not
just any type of relationship, but relationship in its most
sincere, open, nonjudgmental form. Relationship with no other
aim but honest connection and communication between two
individuals.

For this pair of writers, it's been three decades already.
Three decades of arguments, drinking, eating, more discussions,
more plans, philosophizing, bullshitting—and even some talk
about business. Usually, it's just the two of us. Sometimes
girlfriends, wives, and other friends are involved. And did
we mention all the brilliant ideas we've come up with? These
ranged from solving world conflicts to not solving whether
gods exist, to deciding how to run a business, including that
decision we made one night to move our office to a pub one
of us had seen for lease in Nicosia. Our office at the time was
a run-down apartment in the middle of the Cyprus capital.
(And how did an Irishman and an American wind up setting
up a business on this small eastern Mediterranean island?
We'll get to that later, maybe.) But the business was growing,
and we needed more space. And what better than the offices
just above the pub that came with the lease? It was a grand
idea. Yet sadly, it didn't pass Xenophon's test, and we ended up

---

[1]   Martin Buber, *I and Thou*, translated by Ronald Gregor Smith
(Edinburgh, 1962), p. 10.

instead moving to a modern office building just off Archbishop Makarios Avenue—the Cyprus capital's main road, named for the country's first president and religious leader.

The wild thing is that in the end, we made a living out of it. We won't bore you with the details here. We both actually like our work but also put it in its rightful place: work. Not what we are living for. But if there are people in various countries who will pay us for using our brains, our reasoning, our *expertise* (we do hate that word in particular) to help them understand what is happening with the world and how it might affect their commercial and political decisions, then so be it. We actually do a pretty damn good job of it. And some of the topics, at least, have actually been interesting: Clients asked us to provide real-time intelligence and analysis from the 2003 Iraq War (we ran a team of operatives in Iraq for this project in the days leading up to the war and as it progressed over the first few months). We pursued a Russian agent in Central Asia and followed alleged fraudsters literally across the globe— including Donald Trump two decades before he became the U.S. president. And in between, we've had a hand in numerous but much more mundane political and commercial issues that our clients needed investigating.

We always said the ultimate test of whether the business was successful was if it could pay for our eating, drinking, and talking (bullshitting?) sessions. So far, so good. We've done a lot of talking over the years. We hesitate for a moment as we write this, thinking even if for just a brief second, as if we didn't know better: "What will people think, us wasting so much time drinking and talking when we should have been working or at least not wasting time on an idle conversation? There is no real purpose in that, is there? Just chatting away, instead of doing something useful?" That is how it is viewed, sadly, even tragically. A conversation that is not for a specific purpose or aim, that isn't meant to get something or somewhere, is defined as "idle," which is just one way of saying "a waste of time."

But we know better. We sit in a restaurant at lunch, and while the crowd quickly dissipates as the "lunch hour" passes, we enjoy a dessert and coffee and continue to talk. More time passes, and maybe we order another coffee or even cognac if we are in the mood. Time? Usually, at this stage, it is not really a factor, unless there is an afternoon meeting to make. Yes, we can "get away" with this because the business allows it. But that's not the point. The point is that we aren't wasting time with idle talk; long lunches or dinners or whatever setting the conversation may take place in aren't decadent or frivolous. They are essential. They are sometimes empowering and uplifting.

They are potentially life changing and world changing.

Would it be too much to say that our conversations have helped us get where we are today in each of our lives? You can always look at all the banter as just that: bullshit, not important, not related to anything in the "real world," and even if related to something in the "real world," then it doesn't have a "real effect on anything."

That would leave us with the following dichotomy: useful conversation means those that have concrete aims and results, like closing a business deal. And non-useful conversation consists of everything else. Even an example like spilling your heart out to a friend can be thrown into the useful column. Discussions about the weather or the weekend's sports match might be thrown into the "non-useful" category. Yet such materialistic definitions and divisions miss the point.

If we adopt for a moment the language of Buber (and others whom we will discuss later), we suddenly see a third option: conversation defined in terms of a relationship. And not just any type of relationship. The conversation we strive to achieve, in the terminology of Buber, is that of I–You. We look at the other not as a means, but as an equal partner.

Life is complicated. We struggle; it's hard to get up sometimes. Anyone who doesn't admit that isn't in fact living. We strive to find friendship and love. We struggle to find a job and raise our children. We are happy, but we also get depressed. What is it all for? What is my purpose? These are the questions we struggle with every day of our lives, whether we are conscious of it or not. Sometimes these questions explode in front of us. A close relative or friend dies; we lose a job. A business partner cheats us; a personal partner cheats on us. Our children or grandchildren hit rough spots in their lives, and we struggle to help them. Where do we go? What do we do? There is, of course, no single or simple answer.

We were at the Irish pub just off Main Street in Fairfax, Virginia, a few months ago. We had just finished up a day of meetings. A couple of colleagues joined us. It was pretty late—for dreary Fairfax, that means it was after 9 p.m. But it was closer to midnight. We took over a corner of the bar and ordered a round of drinks. We began some idle chatter about the day's work and then segued into some current affairs issues when a guy sitting a couple of bar stools down moved in our direction and joined the conversation. Already weaving, he quickly turned to what was on his mind that night and the reason he was at the bar, drinking by himself. His and his wife had decided to break up. She was staying in the house with the kids. He needed to find somewhere to live. And this had all come down just a couple of hours earlier. He was a wreck. He needed someone to talk to. So we spent the next hour or so listening to his story, trying to cheer him up as best we could and to provide a listening, sympathetic ear. More drinks. More talking. Until we were politely asked to leave the bar—on Main Street in Fairfax, this was way past last call. So we all left and went our separate ways.

Having no one to talk to. Think about it. Scary. Depressing. A sure way to have the life force ripped out of you. Reams have been written about friendship, how important it is to have and maintain friendships. But that has not prevented most of struggling to make and maintain true friends. We know friendships are important. But we still have no friends? Maybe it's just that people have forgotten how vital these bonds are. This is especially so in a world where there is this grand illusion that we are all becoming more and more connected— more connected than ever before in the history of humankind. Of course, this is not an illusion. We actually meet with our parents or grown children only a couple of times a year but speak with them daily (and, nearly as often, "see" them with the help of our phones and computers). We can literally remain in contact with friends and family 24/7, wherever we may be in the world. We always have someone to turn to in a dark hour or to share a happy experience with. Or just to pass the time with. Or do we? "O my friends, there is no friend."[2] Yet let's leave that to cynics, as does Montaigne in his "On Friendship," ripping apart the false friendships built on mutual and even

---

[2] Attibuted to Aristotle in Diogenes Laertius, *Lives and Opinions of Eminent Philosophers* (V, 1, 21) and later quoted by Montaigne, *Essays: On Friendship*, I, 28.

competing interests. He instead proposes an ideal of friendship in which "souls are mingled and confounded in so universal a blending that they efface the seam which joins them together so that it cannot be found."[3]

Maybe that's one thing we are trying to do here: remind ourselves and you, the reader, about the power of friendship. That is undeniably one of the outcomes of our thirty years of talking, working, and having debates about anything and everything that concerned or interested us, that worried us, that made us happy, or that we simply wanted to share or discuss. (And, yes, how discussion, real discussion, opens your eyes to some of the stupid things that cross your mind and whose stupidity only becomes evident when verbalized. But also, conversely, how that idea you weren't sure of can actually be strengthened and grown through dialogue.)

Camaraderie can be developed on a football playing field, at school, in the military, and perhaps even in the workplace. (Don't tell Dilbert.) Bonds are made, even for a lifetime. But there is still another threshold to cross. Shared experiences and interests are not enough. They can provide a basis, but they are not the ultimate in the "binding of souls."

That's where conversation comes in as the foundation of friendship. It brings the ability to really talk to one another about anything—completely open, completely honest. It involves talking but also listening and offering advice and a response—yet not judging. Ulterior motives are put aside, replaced by complete openness and honesty.

---

[3] Michel de Montaigne, *Essays: On Friendship* (London: Penguin Books, 2004), p. 9. The earlier "no friends" quote is from the same essay, with Montaigne attributing to Aristotle.

Have you ever had a conversation like that? Hopefully, the answer is "yes, at least a few."

But why not more? Indeed, we fear that many people out there have never experienced real conversation and don't even know what real conversation is. No, it's not a conversation you initiate because you want something from the person you are speaking to. There is no specific question to be answered, no specific request fulfilled, no favor granted. Real conversation at the most basic level is talking and connecting in a nonjudgmental, undemanding manner. It is the type of communication that at best, you only dream about having with a close friend or family member. Life usually is just too busy for you to engage in such conversations with no immediate purpose or aim. And that is with people close to you, let alone strangers you barely can give the time of day.

If you don't have time for friends, where does that leave strangers? We pass by each other with at best a short hello. More often we simply don't even notice one another. Neighbors with whom we've never spoken. Co-workers we know nothing about and have never tried to know anything about. Relatives whose only relation that is left to us is the exchange of holiday pleasantries. And again friends – maybe they were friends at one time but since then they've been basically forgotten. Or if not forgotten, then there is no more openness, intimacy, or even real concern.

And why be open and honest only with that close friend? Why only with those you feel closest to? Why not with everyone or, at least, widen the circle a little bit? Start honestly listening to others beyond those closest to you. Start honestly talking to them as well. This is the real challenge. It can be hard to really connect with friends, but how much more so with strangers.

We are taught from a young age to be wary of strangers; "others" are to be feared and not trusted. This certainly sounds like a safe way to live, but is it? When you treat people as if they are to be feared, as enemies or potential enemies, then they often become just that. Fences probably don't make for good neighbors, but they certainly don't make for good friends.

Sounds kinda New Age, doesn't it? All this talk of connecting better with others and listening and honesty? If you only knew us personally. We are about as non–New Age as they come. Some would call us downright old fashioned. Indeed, when we mention to friends or family that we are writing a book about conversation, we often get a look of disbelief—they think of us more as "silent-type" guys, definitely not "conversationalists," in the sense of those talkative life-of-the-party types. Feelings? Let's just say that we aren't the kind of guys who talk about them with just anyone. Often, we simply do our best to ignore them ourselves. No one who knows us would ever describe us as people who are "in touch with their feelings."

And let's also get this straight. We aren't even a little bit suggesting that conversation is some sort of magic formula for "saving yourself," let alone the world.

Talking doesn't solve everything, and it alone can't address everything at personal level or at the political level. Every problem can't be "talked through." Sometimes there is no choice but to get up and leave the table and resort to other means. So, yes, give peace a chance. And negotiated resolutions are surely preferable. But beware of giving the other cheek. Bad people exist who will take advantage of your Christian charity, to the point where you might not have another cheek to give again, ever.

Real conversation is robust and perhaps even life changing—but not always. And even when it is, that's because it's part of a larger process.

So, what can conversation do, on a personal level? Expand your horizons and knowledge, help clarify your thoughts and feelings, and even make life more meaningful by helping you focus on what is really important.

And what can conversation do for our world? It will make or break it. It's that simple: As conversation dies, so does one of the most elementary qualities of humanity—reason. When we are engaged in a real discussion, we are thinking. When we aren't—and nowadays we (as in the human species) mostly are not—we are either silent or engaged in something that pretends to be a conversation but really isn't.

We understand that we are contradicting ourselves. How can we say in the same breath (or in the same chapter) that we don't advocate conversation as some kind of magical solution to our and the world's problems, but then also say conversation can be life changing? How can we speak of a conversation that is not a real conversation?

The answer is easy. Or, should we say, it should be easy: Life is complicated, and so are humans. People want straightforward answers; no "gray areas" allowed. You are either with us or against us; you must take sides and never change sides. Forget about "sinner repent." Today, once seen as a sinner, you will always be seen in that light. "To err is human; to forgive divine," is no longer the ideal. Forgiveness and repentance are no longer the fashion; passing judgment is. For when there is no conversation, there is no forgiveness; there is no understanding of the Other; we see only Us and Them.

So, do we think things are bad today, in an age when conversation is crushed on the Left by political correctness on steroids and on the Right by fascism disguised as patriotism? It was nearly eighty years ago when one of the greatest advocates of rational thought in the twentieth century, Bertrand Russell, had his appointment to Professor of Philosophy at City College in New York rescinded because the idea that we should let reason run free was considered not just radical but also unacceptable. Then and now, critical thinking was feared.

Perhaps Russell was lucky. Socrates was put to death for similar views. And in the interim 2,500 years, other freethinkers have similarly suffered simply for wanting to carry out real conversation, testing their own opinions and those of others to the fullest extent possible. As Russell put it in his 1927 London lecture, "Why I Am Not a Christian":

> We want to stand upon our own feet and look fair and square at the world—its good facts, its bad facts, it beauties, and its ugliness; see the world as it is, and not be no afraid of it. Conquer the world by intelligence, and not by being slavishly subdued by the terror that comes from it.[4]

Russell was right on the mark. Nearly a century later, terror still rules too widely. When Russell wrote, "Conquer the world by intelligence, and not merely by being slavishly subdued

---

[4] Bertrand Russell, *"Why I Am Not a Christian" and Other Essays on Religion and Related Subjects*, edited by Paul Edwards (London: Unwin Books, 1957), p. 26.

by the terror that comes from it," he was not referring to the terror arising from religion or dictatorship per se—although there is certainly a correlation. Instead, Russell was pointing to the human tendency to fear freedom—in particular, freedom of thought—and instead to prefer to hold onto dogmas and beliefs that provide comfort and reassurance. People are too often terrified of testing their theories and ideas. They prefer false traditions and beliefs, even when these are clearly detrimental to themselves and their loved ones, over reasoned answers. Indeed, no amount of reason can change a mind barricaded by walls built of prejudice and fear. The atmosphere of intellectual terror Russell first described between the world wars, which got him thrown out of an American university in 1940, continues to reign in many quarters today.

The choice is simple: societies and individuals guided by intelligence or by terror. How have we allowed ourselves to degenerate into a world of simple black and white? Why can't we hold to the words of the late Nobel Prize–winning physicist Niels Bohr: "There are two sorts of truth: profound truths recognized by the fact that the opposite is also a profound truth, in contrast to trivialities where opposites are obviously absurd."[5] Ponder that for a moment. Profound truths are those whose opposites are also correct. Trivial truths are those whose opposites are obviously absurd! Bohr and Einstein discovered quantum mechanics, though Einstein at first did not accept much of Bohr's theorizing. Eventually, he was convinced. Their lifelong conversations—not necessarily as friends but as fellow scientists with overlapping interests—are a powerful example

---

[5]   Niels Bohr, as quoted by his son Hans Bohr, in *My Father Niels Bohr: His Life and Work* (1967), p. 328.

of where dialogue can take us. Einstein disagreed but listened and explained his reservations. Bohr explained his viewpoints, and Einstein eventually joined him. Such great thinkers were open to conversation, despite their differences, and we aren't. How absurd is that?

We aren't harking back to some Utopian period or "good old days." Real conversations always faced a great struggle and continue to. And the battle was often a bloody one. Buber and Russell were exceptions in their respective societies. They fought for people to free their minds but, in honest analysis, clearly failed to achieve this on a large scale. They provided ammunition for like-minded people, but clearly not enough. Think of the potential and power of looking at the world as Bohr did—being open to the possibility that certain profound truths allow for their opposites to also be profoundly true. The intellectual sky no longer has any limits. Human creativity is set free. The conversation is no longer dull and even worse angry but instead invigorating and inspiring. You are no longer searching to prove the other wrong and show her you are correct.

Drop the capital "T" from truth. It may be a little scary at first, a little discomfiting. The capital "T" is undoubtedly easier to hang on to. Yet it more often just crushes you. Choose truth over Truth. Stop thinking in black and white, us and them. And let the conversation begin.

> I know that I am mortal, ephemeral; yet
> when I track the
>   Clustering spiral orbits of the stars
>   My feet touch earth no longer: a
> heavenly nursling,

Ambrosia-filled, I company with
God.[6]

"Ptolemy's words are a reminder that for the Greeks
spirituality and rationality, mythos and logos, could co-exist
without conflict," explained Charles Freeman, in his scathing
critique of Christianity's effect on Western thinking, *The
Closing of the Western Mind: The Rise of Faith and the Fall of
Reason.*[7]

As we have seen, one of the most sophisticated of the
Greek intellectual achievements was the distinction between
areas of knowledge in which certainty was possible and those
that were not subject to rationalism. A mathematical proof
could be sustained by deductive logic and was unarguably
true, while a myth was fluid and flexible, open to individual
interpretation. To the Greeks, the idea that anyone could insist
that others respect the truth of a myth was absurd, yet this did
not mean that a myth lacked power. Whether used to explain
or justify a ritual or as a means to explore issues in tragic drama,
myth was a crucial way of mediating between the real and the
imagined worlds. The mature mind, as Aristotle had stressed,
was one in which reason and emotion could be sustained in
harmony.[8]

The fluidity in thinking that Ancient Greece permitted
was the impetus for the flourishing of intellectual thought,
the sciences, and the spiritual. Freeman, in *The Closing of the*

---

[6] Ptolemy, as quoted in Charles Freeman, *The Closing of the Western
Mind: The Rise of Faith and the Fall of Reason* (London: Pimlico,
2003), p. 13.

[7] Ibid.

[8] Ibid., pp. 65–66.

Western Mind, points to how the Ancient Greeks saw the world of humans and the world of the gods as interchangeable, the gods and humans actively involved in each other's worlds and having intimate relations, as well as humans even transforming into gods. From the Greek and later Roman perspectives, this worldview made more understandable the Christian belief that Jesus was a deity, as well as the son of God. Zeus and Apollo had children. Just a few centuries before Jesus, Alexander of Macedonia laid claim to much of the Greek-known world, declaring himself a son of Zeus.

Faith and Reason were complementary and not competitive. They could live side by side. They each knew their place. And perhaps most important, the Ancient Greek leaders recognized the importance of both Faith and Reason or the worlds of mythos and logos. The young Alexander the Great, as he made his way through Egypt and Persia in his conquests, adopted the local gods and even made them his own. He understood their importance to the local peoples now coming under his rule. There was an understanding of the place of mythos in society. Beliefs—indeed, multiple gods and traditions—lived side by side, along with a culture that encouraged rational thought and inquiry.

But that was to change. As Freeman points out, less than five hundred years after the birth of Jesus, as Christianity began to take hold in the Roman Empire, Greek rationalism and creativity were being stamped out in Europe. Faith—and not reason—was seen as what was required for the advancement of society. And not the multiple religions of the Greek and early Roman empires, but only the one Christian faith. Other faiths were attacked. And Reason was attacked. Freeman quotes Augustine to drive the point home: "There is another form of temptation, even more fraught with danger. This is the disease of curiosity ... It is this which drives us to try and discover the secrets of nature, those secrets which are beyond our understanding, which can avail us nothing and which man should not wish to learn."[9]

The conversation Socrates had begun with his pupils at the Athens Lyceum was over. In the Holy Roman Empire, the pupils learned to listen and obey, not to enter into conversation and explore.

We may wince when we read of Augustine describing the "disease of curiosity," but our reaction is not an honest one. Ours is a world considerably evolved since the early days of the Holy Roman Empire, but it is still a world where beliefs trump facts. And not only religion is to blame. Freeman points out that the attempt by the Church to come to terms with rational thinking, as reflected in the works of Thomas Aquinas, was doomed to failure. Reason can never lead to "theological truths," he argues, without, however, at least openly noting the oxymoronic meaning of the term itself.[10] Aquinas's attempt to align religious belief with rational thought may have "collapsed in the Enlightenment," and Reason's hand strengthened. But the battle was far from over. Reason soon faced not only religious attacks but also an ongoing onslaught by ideologies of various forms from across the cultural and political spectrum. Each claims to hold the Answer, rejecting all others and demanding allegiance, even if it must be enforced by violence. The "isms" have come and gone, then come back with new faces. Their trails are streaked in blood. Reason, too, has taken such

---

[9]   Ibid., Augustine quote included before the introduction.
[10]   Ibid., p. 340.

a battering that some believe rational thinking has a terminal illness. The American philosopher Alan Bloom was referring to his country as a whole and not merely academia when he wrote, "The differences and the indifferences are too great. It is difficult to imagine that there is either the wherewithal or the energy within the university to constitute or reconstitute the idea of an educated human being and establish a liberal education again."[11] This was in 1987, more than a decade before Freeman's book with a similar name. Freeman's perspective was historic; Bloom's was a critique of the times. Yet the message resonates to this day. Rational thought is at risk. Bloom was addressing specifically the state of American universities, but his message was to American society as a whole. That was how the book was received—a scathing and powerful critique of American culture.

"This is the American moment in world history, the one for which we will forever be judged. Just as in politics the responsibility for the fate of freedom in the world has devolved upon our regime, so the fate of philosophy in the world has devolved upon our universities, and the two are related as they have never been before. The gravity of our given task is great, and it is very much in doubt how the future will judge our stewardship."[12]

Bloom can perhaps be excused for his American-centered perspective. He was writing at a time of unparalleled U.S. political and economic dominance. He recognized that his country was at the height of its power and influence but, despite

---

[11] Allan Bloom, *The Closing of the American Mind* (New York: Simon and Schuster, 1987), p. 380.

[12] Ibid., p. 382.

this, was failing in the most fundamental task of developing a well-educated society. And he recognized that as the country's education system failed, along with it society's bulwark of reason and rationality would collapse.

> The real community of man is the community of those who seek the truth, of the potential knowers, that is, in principle, of all men to the extent they desire to know.[13]

---

[13] Ibid., p. 381.

02

Pass the Chardonnay

The time to stop talking is when
the other person nods his head
affirmatively but says nothing.
— Henry S. Haskins

*I*T'S EASY TO observe how conversations end. Like old soldiers, they don't die; they just fade away—usually into a jumble of non sequiturs, repetitions, and what-abouts. That's if they don't end with a bang—an angry shout, a fist crashed on the table, a door slammed. Beginnings are more obscure because of their littleness (small talk) or their apparent insignificance before they expand into earnest diversions and disagreements. People in conversation are followers of Yogi Berra's advice: "When you come to a fork in the road, take it!" Here's a delightful portrait of the start of a conversation:

> I was sitting with my friend Robi at the
> Cafe Central in Budapest when the subject
> turned to religion and the Enlightenment,
> namely about the separation of God from

moral systems. The topic was a poor choice.
We had discussed it before in various forms
and quickly came to a stalemate. There
was an awkward silence. A young man sat
down at the adjoining table and ordered
an espresso in English. Robi and I were
speaking Hungarian. "Should we ask our
new neighbor the Enlightenment question?"
I asked. Robi nodded noncommittally as
the neighbor picked up his smartphone.
I laid out what could happen: one, the
conversation could be short and awkward;
two, it could be long and superficial; three,
it could be long and not superficial. The
likelihood of one or two was very high, I
submitted. Robi nodded, unimpressed, and
deepened the awkward silence.

"Excuse me. Do you mind if I ask whether you have any
views on the Enlightenment?"
"What do you mean?"
"The Enlightenment 18th century, Voltaire, Kant."
"Yes. What about it?"
"We were discussing the Enlightenment's separation of
moral systems from God," I explained. "Pluses and minuses," I
added, trying not to poison the well.
"Good or bad, it had to happen," said our neighbor, with
an accent now identifiable as Spanish. "It's evolution."[14]

---

[14] Holly A. Case, *The Enlightenment Question*, 3 Quarks Daily.

We were sitting at the Family Nest Restaurant in Nicosia when the subject turned to artificial intelligence, a subject we had discussed previously, but we usually came to a stalemate because of our profound ignorance of the latest research.

"Waiter," one of us said, "please uncork the Chardonnay."

Thomas: I'll predict for you that when computerized artificial intelligence becomes self-aware, it won't think, *Okay, my mission in this brave new world where machines are in full control is to search for wisdom.* It will hunt for more knowledge and data, facts about the universe, and tips on how an AI can control the world. You think an AI is going to sit there and think, *Now, how should I love my neighbor in Apple and not hate my neighbor in Google?*

Bill: I'm trying to be sympathetic to artificial intelligence. But also to identify its limitations. So I'm all for AI being used to supplement my poor memory and even poorer retention of knowledge. Go ahead and put in that implant, which will give my brain instant access to Wikipedia-like knowledge. But wisdom—that's something we will never be able to expect from AI.

Thomas: Can you tell me why I need this so-called wisdom? It doesn't exist. What I need is knowledge. If I didn't have knowledge of, say, how to organize and run your website, your company might collapse. I need knowledge, so I can function as a colleague, a member of the community, and help Bill's company, as well as earn income for my family. I surely do need knowledge. Why do I need fucking wisdom as well?

Bill: Okay, I'll give you a good reason. I won't call it *knowledge* or *wisdom.* I'll put the terms aside. A friend comes to you one day and says, "I'm depressed. I'm scared I might even hurt myself. I don't know what to do. I don't know how to deal with it."

Thomas: Jesus, couldn't you think of a gloomier example? Bad karma! But if you must, this is not a case for wisdom or knowledge or advice. It's a case for empathy, support, understanding, whatever. But first, action.

Bill: You need someone who can advise a person how he or she can get through this. That is what you need.

Thomas: But you wouldn't call a friend first. You'd need to call a psychiatrist (one who is a scientist, not a babbler) or a depression hotline, someone who can take immediate knowledgeable action. Those are people with knowledge.

Bill: They don't know shit. They have no wisdom.

Thomas: They have knowledge; they have the tools to take urgent action. And soon, a robot's algorithm will know what to do, and you'll be wise to heed it. Apart from that, wisdom's mostly crap.

Bill: Okay, I get it. The example of my depressed friend was a bad one. But think of all the times I've come to you with ideas, questions I've been thinking about, whether personal or business related. Questions that have no easy answers and, in fact, probably have no "right" or "wrong" answers. Not questions you can figure out by doing a few Google searches or even an infinite number of them.

* * * * * *

For Alan Bloom, though he does not say it outright, it would appear conversation in its highest form is an ideal that can be sought but is difficult to obtain. For him, this ideal

ﺍ

is exemplified in what he describes as the true friendship of Plato and Aristotle: "Their common concern for the good linked them; their disagreement about it proved they needed one another to understand it."[15] How masterfully Bloom fuses together the apparent anomaly that, in fact, is at the heart of true friendship and true conversation—it isn't just about the things they agree on, but it celebrates their differences. The differences are respected and not belittled. Both men are confident that while their paths might be different, they have the same aim in mind.

They are absolutely one soul, as they look at the problem. This, according to Plato, is the only true friendship, the only real common good. It is here where people find the contact they so desperately seek. The other kinds of relatedness are only imperfect reflections of true friendship; they try to be self-sustaining, but they gain their only justification from their ultimate relation to this—to true friendship itself. That is the meaning of the riddle of the improbable philosopher-kings the philosophers dreamed of. They have a true community that is exemplary among all other communities.

This is a radical teaching but perhaps one appropriate for our own radical time, in which proximate attachments have become so questionable, and we know of no others.[16]

In this book, our aim is much less ambitious, in many respects. We have no potential misconceptions about where philosophers and kings stand in our society. But like Bloom, we see "the contact people desperately seek." The contact that we consider here begins in a conversation, sometimes in a bar, a

---

[15] Ibid., p. 381.
[16] Ibid., pp. 381–382.

coffee shop, a conference room, or wherever people meet—real people like us.

Of course, most conversation is empty and meaningless. *Merriam-Webster* defines conversation as the "oral exchange of sentiments, observations, opinions or ideas." The dictionary then further elaborates through a literary quote: "[W]e had talk enough but no conversation; there was nothing discussed." For Samuel Johnson, the source of the citation, conversation is an intellectual process, and that is what separates it from passing banter.

We argue in this book that real conversation is different from common, day-to-day dialogue not just in content, but also in intent. Though it is different from idle banter, we nevertheless engage in it without trying to achieve some material end. Real conversation is both a means and an end in itself.

We also argue that real conversation gives back: conversation makes you a better person.

Real conversation lies on the cusp between reason and emotion. It includes both the rational and the spiritual. It recognizes, as did the Ancient Greeks, that there is a place for both logos and mythos; the rational and the spiritual are not enemies. Both are elements of what makes us human.

The main adversaries of Real Conversation: Those who claim they know what is True and Right and demand that we all acquiesce to their view. They refuse to partake in conversation because they believe they already have all the Answers. There is no room for dialogue.

The problem is not ignorance. Ignorance can be bliss when it leads us to question everything and take nothing for granted, and to be wary of those who claim they know what is True and Right. We realize we are largely ignorant. But that is why we must keep asking questions, as well as explore, research, and investigate. We talk. We listen. We understand that we must not blindly believe but must listen to and explore the ideas of others, as well as our own. In this way, we are open to real conversation.

Conversation is at its very essence a meeting. It is connection even before dialogue enters the equation. Connection and empathy. A recognition of the Other, of the Other not just as a separate being but as someone significant, someone who should be respected and listened to. The words that are exchanged are important, but so, too, are the feelings that one opens up to in the Other. Buber wrote a small book late in life that could be the closest to autobiographical of any of his works. In it, he describes short vignettes of significant events in his life. *Meetings*, as the book is titled, includes about a dozen short stories of encounters that shaped his life. For a man who lived through two world wars, immigrated to Palestine, and became a renowned philosopher and theologian, one might expect that he would choose major or traumatic instances in his life. Instead, however, he gives us simple encounters—with his parents as a child and with a teacher, a fellow intellectual, a fellow theologian, a pupil—that shaped his life. His message is as profound as it is clear: "All real living is meeting."

Ponder this simple statement for a moment. Recognize the challenge Buber is presenting. He differentiates living from real living. It is real living that humans should strive for. We need to recognize the significance and power of the encounters with people who make up our lives when we open ourselves up to truly connect with them. Buber challenges humankind: Stop just living; you have the potential to really live by truly opening yourself up to others.

One thing we want to get straight from the outset. We aren't about pompous philosophizing or pontificating. We aren't just two privileged old white guys with nothing better to do than make shallow claims about life and what it means for us, as if anyone should care. We will tell you more about ourselves later. Yet it is essential to understand from the outset that while we admit we don't have the Answers to anything, the struggle to understand ourselves and the world around us is a struggle of every human, no matter how rich or poor, which continent he or she lives on, or any of the infinite number of things that make us different.

That struggle for meaning and understanding is common to us all. And conversation, the kind of honest and open conversation we advocate for here, is an essential tool in that struggle.

The struggle for meaning and understanding is not for the privileged few. At universities, think tanks, centers of scientific research and study, and countless other organizations and institutions around the world, people indeed may be searching for truth. We don't belittle this. We have the utmost respect and appreciation for these efforts. Humankind's collective memory is pathetically short. How quickly have we forgotten the bloody struggle of reason against the darkness of superstition and religion, at least as it used to display itself and in many circles still does? That struggle continues. As does the struggle of each of us to find our place in the world.

The conversation isn't just about us. The conversation is about our world. It is about our future.

The choice is ours: Is our future one of silence? Or is it of conversation? Silence ends in ignorance; conversation, in enlightenment. It would appear to be an easy choice, but it isn't. Indeed, as we move well into the twenty-first century, we look around in astonishment at how many people have chosen silence and how few, conversation. Yet we know in our hearts that it is no surprise. Real conversation—the ability to open oneself up to others, to their thoughts and feelings—has never been a "natural" characteristic of humans. Indeed, our history is one of repeatedly choosing darkness: the darkness of silencing others and caring only for ourselves and those we identify as being like us.

We've wandered a bit from Xenophon, but perhaps that's the point. Conversation wanders. That is one of the joys of a good conversation. It gets more intense, only to suddenly veer off in a new direction. We may lose our way. Yet if we always have conversation, real conversation, to return to, everything will be alright.

03

Yes, There Are Rules

*Half the world is composed of people
who have something to say and can't,
and the other half who have nothing
to say and keep on saying it.*
—Robert Frost

IN THE MODERN world, every conversation has the potential to evolve into an argument. The most trivial issue can set someone screaming for and against it. The British traditionally used to stick to the weather as a topic. Even that has become a minefield in the clash between climate change deniers and those who respect scientific evidence. American broadcaster and TED-talks guru Celeste Headlee has compiled ten rules for good conversations, which she outlines in her lectures:

"There's a lot of advice around on this," she says. "Things like looking a person in the eye, leaning forward, nodding your head, and so on. Forget all that. It's crap. There is no reason to learn how to show you're paying attention if you are in fact—you know, paying attention."

Here are her rules:

Number one: Don't multitask. Be present, put away your phone, stop thinking about dinner.

Number two: Don't pontificate. You're not Wikipedia. As Bill Nye said, "Everyone you'll ever meet knows something that you don't."

Number three: Use open-ended questions. Journalists get it right with questions that ask "who, what, where, when, why."

Number four: Go with the flow. Irrelevant facts and opinions will come into your mind; you need to let them go out of your mind, not out of your mouth.

Number five: If you don't know, say that you don't know. You're not Wikipedia.

Number six: Don't undermine their experience with yours. Don't do, "Yeah, that happened to me " It didn't. Every person's experience and reaction is unique.

Number seven: Don't repeat yourself. It's condescending and really boring.

Number eight: Stay out of the weeds. We don't care about all those interrupting details, what day it was, the time, the exact place, Aunt Susie, or was it Jane?

Number nine: The most important one. (Yes, it's numbered nine—we were just building up to it.) Listen! Mostly, we don't listen with the intent to understand—we listen with the intent to reply. Calvin Coolidge said, "No one ever listened their way out of a job."

Number ten: Be brief.

"Human speech is like a cracked kettle on which we tap crude rhythms for bears to dance to, while we long to make music that will melt the stars," wrote Gustave Flaubert in

Madame Bovary. The pleasure we can take in completely banal chats with people we like is the pleasure of talking itself. When the experts debate modern conversation or where it's headed, they also ponder what we might do to save it from death by digital assault. It's astonishing how many books, articles, and videos are out there (yes, in the digital world) admonishing us to cast the devil's devices aside and talk to one another again.

The only consistent advice on the topic comes wrapped in that one word (Number nine, above): *listen.* Listen to other people, listen to learn something about their world. Lose yourself, find them. And beware of pretending to listen—it's not a space for thinking about what you're going to say next or wondering what to get for dinner. From good listening comes good questions to ask, adding curiosity and empathy. "Everyone you ever meet knows something you don't—people are fascinating, but only if you're interested in them do you learn why," Headlee says. Back to Alice:

Hatter: Your hair wants cutting.
Alice: You should learn not to make personal remarks. It's very
    rude.
Hatter: Why is a raven like a writing-desk?
Alice: I believe I can guess that.
Hatter: Do you mean that you think you can find out the
    answer to it?
Alice: Exactly so.
March Hare: Then you should say what you mean.
Alice: I do! At least—at least I mean what I say—that's the
    same thing, you know.
Hatter: Not the same thing a bit!

March Hare: You might just as well say that "I like what I get" is the same thing as "I get what I like"!

So, why is a raven like a writing desk? There is no answer to that; Lewis Carroll said so many times. But answer is this:

Why is a good conversation like a miniskirt? Easy!

It's short enough to maintain interest but long enough to cover the subject.

A good conversation, even a simple one, can change your life. So can a miniskirt. Here's a true story. Let's do Chaucer; let's call these snippets "tales."

THOMAS: THE PRIEST'S TALE

When I write a memoir, I need to include conversations I have had—and then, I am unable to recall any of them with clarity. Childhood conversations were monologues: parents issuing orders or ranting over some transgression. Conversations with other kids also seem to have been monologues but internal ones: talking to myself and not listening to the other person. This may be the most intolerable social habit we carry into adulthood. We still have conversations where we give the appearance of listening to our companions, but we are composing what we want to say when the other person shuts up for a second. The author Dame Rebecca West said, "There is no such thing as conversation. It is an illusion. There are intersecting monologues. That is all."

The first conversation I recall with pleasure and clarity happened when I was seventeen, so already almost an adult. It was a simple conversation, and it changed my life. Now that's a good conversation.

I was a year into studying at a Jesuit seminary in a medieval castle in the west of Ireland and was already questioning my decision to go there. I had convinced myself my doubts were philosophical. The Catholic concept of teaching philosophy at that time halted somewhere in the thirteenth century with the arrival of scholasticism. The writings of antiquity had been rediscovered. It disturbed the church to watch the thoughts of Plato, Socrates, and Aristotle encroaching on their sacred beliefs with nary a nod to Jesus. The robust, non-superstitious, and wide-ranging philosophies of the Greeks were a threat. Thomas Aquinas and Augustine were admirers of the Greeks but felt obliged to corral their wisdom into a Christian paddock. It was deemed essential to reconcile Christian theology with classical philosophy, especially that of Aristotle. After Thomas Aquinas wrote his *Summa Theologiae*—and after he reconciled Aristotle and the Bible and declared that reason is to be found in God—the church considered the job done. So there! Any further pagan philosophical speculation would be heresy, the work of Satan and not scholars.

I was an arrogant teenage philosophy student (and thus an expert), and I decided this was intolerable. Were we to dump and ignore anyone of interest who down the centuries had added their copious footnotes to the Socratics, Platonists, Stoics, and Epicureans? Well, I was having none of that and would have a word with the seminary's father superior about it.

Then, around this time of philosophical epiphany, I experienced another crisis of faith. Every afternoon we students took a break from studies and prayers to stroll the monastery gardens in groups of four. We had to speak in Latin to improve our proficiency—an exercise known as *colloquium*, Latin for "conversation." This was just before the Vatican II council dumped Latin as the obligatory language of Catholic ritual. The garden in the castle grounds was ancient and delightful, its path lined with primroses and pansies that wound through a dense wood. (Sorry, Dante.) One September afternoon I was walking the walk and talking the colloquium with three English students. They were struggling to find a Latin vocabulary to discuss their home soccer teams, a topic of no interest to me, and so I remained silent.

Without warning, the woodland path became a road to Damascus. There was no blinding light, but there was a vision. Beside the path, some fifty meters away, was an old-fashioned stone well, complete with a winch, a rope, and a bucket to drop into the clear spring water below. I'd never seen it used before. But now, bent over the well, letting down the bucket, was a girl with long red hair and a pretty white dress. It was the 1960s, and unbeknownst to us, the miniskirt had arrived in Ireland. The immediate image was to me more innocent and angelic, a thing of beauty, rather than anything sexual. Yet it was clear later—"emotion recollected in tranquility"—that the fierce emotional shock I felt was far from religious or aesthetic. To hell with the problems of Catholic philosophy. There was also the problem of Catholic celibacy.

A few days later, I saw from my room window that the father superior was strolling on the front lawn in front of the castle. I slipped downstairs and approached him.

"May I have a word, Father?"

"Yes, Frater," he said and motioned me to a wooden bench. It was a sunny September evening, scenic and mild. Neither of us spoke for a few minutes. Father Bradley was around sixty, a tall and broad man with a large flat face that bore the battered scars of a distant accident. He had gone through the window of a car that crashed in Australia a couple of decades earlier. The driver had died—it was the era before seat belts. Unproven rumors hinted it was a woman.

"Do you remember your first novitiate days?" I asked him.

"Not as well as I remember some other things," he said dryly, probably a reference to his near-death experience.

"What I mean is—do you remember having doubts about choosing to be a priest?"

"I've never stopped having doubts, if you must know. I don't remember my specific thoughts at the seminary, but they've always been there. There is nothing wrong with doubt. It is certainty that causes the most trouble. Certainty is what Socrates meant by an unexamined life."

He paused and looked at me, raising an eyebrow to check whether I wanted to speak. I didn't.

"So you have doubts about being here?"

"Yes. Not consistent, but they come and sometimes are strong."

"All that matters is how you act. Thoughts, doubts, questions—all are as fickle and duplicitous as dreams. Are yours solid doubts about the faith or disguised longings for other ways of life? Homesickness?"

Other ways of life. There she is again in my mind's eye—red hair, white mini, a fringe of white panties. I sighed and waved my hand toward the fields, the river, and the copse.

"I enjoy the studies," I said. "But I feel how the beautiful things of the world are very beautiful, and I miss them."

"Look, you're a very smart young man, and I'm too old for platitudes. I cannot help you. You're here by choice. You can stay by choice; you can leave by choice. You must walk with your doubts, examine them when they come. But do not try to fool yourself. You could fool me or your tutors, but you cannot fool God. And if you fool yourself, you will know you're doing it. Thoughts are only thoughts and are useless until they guide you to actions. Knowledge is not wisdom, piety is not faith, words are not deeds. Learn the difference in these things. Study, think, pray; then act."

He looked at me keenly with some kindness in his battered face.

"You will be an asset to the Jesuits, and we would be sorry to lose you. Yes, the beautiful things of the world are very beautiful. But are they enough? It is for you to decide."

We rose from the bench together, the conversation ended, and walked back to the hall in silence.

A month later, I was gone. I couldn't fool a god I no longer believed in. I never returned to the castle or to religion. Four years later, I was flying Vulcan nuclear bombers in the British Royal Air Force.

Yes, that was one life-changing conversation.

BILL: THE STUDENT'S TALE

Sometimes it is the conversations of which we are largely witnesses that have greatest impact.

I remember well my time at the University of Chicago. I admit that among the strongest of my memories were the bitter cold winters. The wind and cold felt like they were literally burning any exposed part of my body, as I made it across the Midway from the dorms on the South Side and classes in

Hyde Park. There were also the gunshots we sometimes heard at night in the dorms because then, like now, crime was out of control in Chicago. I arrived in Chicago after taking a gap year after high school, which included travel in Europe. I came back a little apprehensive about fitting in and also still torn by the fact that Chicago was not among my top choices of schools but the only good one to which I was accepted. Yet then, like now, I was somewhat of a geek when it came to enjoying learning and was ready for the academic rigor Chicago entailed, in particular after having taken the year off.

I knew coming in that Chicago had a different approach to Freshman Year. There were no big introductory classes, similar to most universities in the United States. Instead, there were small seminars primarily taught by top faculty. These were all discussion classes, no long boring lectures. You had to come prepared to class and ready to debate/discuss the lesson topics. I was and am fairly shy and not very well spoken, so for the most part I just listened. What a show! And that grew more intense because I knew I might be called on at any moment. I particularly enjoyed the philosophy seminar, which was more like a Great Books of Western Civilization class. But again, it was all discussion, led by a brilliant (and I remember also quite old, white-haired) professor.

It was the Socratic method on full display—although at the time I didn't realize it. What I witnessed was this incredible back and forth, a clash of minds and ideas, perhaps juvenile, given our age and education (or lack thereof). Yet our old professor treated us as equals. He didn't tell us what to think. He just kept challenging us with more questions, brilliantly leading the conversation forward.

We started with Genesis and took an entire class for just the first few chapters. He dwelled on the Garden of Eden scene. "What was that fruit Adam and Eve ate?" The new students struggled to remember. "It doesn't say," answered one student. The professor deftly moved the discussion forward, and I felt as if I myself were taking a bite of the forbidden fruit. I began to realize the significance of just what it meant by "the tree of the knowledge of good and evil." I suppose I have only myself to blame; I hadn't been listening well enough as a kid at Hebrew school. No, we weren't talking about a tasty apple Adam wanted a bite of, despite being forbidden by God. This wasn't just a story of disobedience. The message was much greater and more significant, as I was beginning to learn. Here my eyes were opened to what I had taken as a routine and mundane story that all of a sudden actually hit at the heart of the human condition, at least as I was beginning to understand it at the time. Adam and Eve had stood before the Tree of the Knowledge of Good and Evil and all that it symbolized. There could be life ignorant of good and evil, or life with knowledge of good and evil. There was thus also good and evil but, of course, also the possibility that there indeed were no such things, as well as an infinite number of possibilities in between. What fun! What a geek?

I fell in love in Chicago, with books. But as a lover, I was less than faithful. In Chicago, I fell for all things philosophical. Yet it was only a year later, fleeing the bitter cold of Chicago and heading east to a new school, this time in New York City, that I discovered the Russians and, in particular, Dostoevsky. I still could not commit, though, and by the next year, back in my home state at the University of Virginia and its small Comparative Literature Department, my eyes were really opened to all that literature and reading and criticism had to offer. It was a fun ride those four years.

Even so, it ended pretty abruptly. I'm not really sure why. Certainly, it was no conscious decision. I did still pick up a book from time to time. I suppose life is simply to blame. After leaving university and entering the "real world," I basically forgot my first love (despite all the hours we spent together, mainly in the libraries of Chicago, New York City, and finally Charlottesville), only to find her again much later in life.

04

Mountains and Molehills

The struggle itself towards the heights
is enough to fill a man's heart.
One must imagine Sisyphus happy.
—Albert Camus

$\mathcal{T}$HE 900-METER HIKE up to the top of Saint Hilarion Castle in the Kyrenia Mountain Range in northern Cyprus is a little rough at points. But not as rough as the meaningless daily mountain hike of the Greek loser Sisyphus, of whom more shortly.

You already feel like you're in for a special surprise, as you drive up from a pass on the highway through the mountain range linking the capital of Nicosia in the plains below with the ancient port of Kyrenia. As you gain elevation, you get your first peek at the Mediterranean coastline. Unlike on the southern Greek side of the island of Cyprus, in the north the coastline remains largely undeveloped. This is perhaps the only good impact of the Turkish invasion and occupation. Most countries enforce strict trade and financial restrictions on the Turkish-occupied north, an entity only Turkey recognizes as a state. With a few exceptions, the only planes that land at the area's small "international" airport are from Turkey. Sanctions also hamper foreign investment. There are a few high-end casinos catering to Russian and Eastern European customers and several new residential developments by foreigners willing to take the risk of investing in the occupied areas, given the relatively low prices. In recent years, more tourists are also arriving, now that there are several border crossing points between the south and the north.

Cyprus is one of the world's forgotten conflict zones. Forgotten in part because although the country is divided, UN peacekeeping forces are stationed along the barbed-wire border, and for the last three decades all has been relatively quiet. During the Turkish invasion in 1974 and its immediate aftermath, however, this area endured fighting, casualties, and an onslaught of more than 200,000 refugees from both sides (i.e. ., both Greek and Turkish Cypriot). In recent years, there have even been attempts to reunify the island and bring about at least some level of normalization between the sides—for instance, at the border crossings. When things are quiet, as they've been for many years now, they tend to lose the world's attention—especially when considering a small island in the eastern Mediterranean, even if it's strategically located.

It is the island's strategic location that is the backdrop of our hike in the Kyrenia Mountains. The castle is one of several on the islands, remnants of earlier civilizations and armies that—understanding the importance of Cyprus's location— laid claim to the island. Saint Hilarion was an obscure hermit who fled to Cyprus after Arabs conquered the Holy Land in the seventh century, and he built a hermitage on this peak of the Kyrenia Mountains. The location has commanding views of the mountain pass from Kyrenia to Nicosia, as well as of the Nicosia central plain and Kyrenia harbor. Inevitably, Hilarion's strategic position attracted the attention of military commanders down the millennia until the present. It became the most important in a string of castles along the narrow mountain ridge, along with Buffavento and Kantara. The Byzantines first fortified Hilarion in the eleventh century, and the Crusader Lusignans later upgraded it, adding royal summer-residence wings. Venice occupied the castle until the Turks conquered Cyprus in the sixteenth century.

We parked at the foothill of Hilarion and, with a friend and a young family member, started making our way up. The view was picture-perfect. The Turkish mainland lay in the far distance. Forests covered much of the mountain range. Below, the coastline and blue seas beckoned. The atmosphere was enchanting. History, nature, geography, clashes of civilizations old and new, all mixed together. The excitement of the hike awaited us, although looking ahead we also discovered awaiting us a steep incline, then farther up the castle walls, and even higher the lookout posts.

What an incredible world! How lucky we were. As youngsters, one of us in suburban Virginia, the other in the small Irish town in Tipperary, we wouldn't have even been able to dream of such an adventure. We were now worlds away from our original homes, with friends we discovered as we became adults and ventured out in the world. Such experiences leave their mark with you as warm memories. They are also strong enough at the time to give you pause. Yes, the pause was partly to catch our breath when we reached the top of the highest watchtower. The hot afternoon sun had taken its toll on the hike up, but we could already feel a cool evening breeze-off the sea below. The mountain range crossing the island was laid out before us. In the near distance were a small Turkish army outpost and a shooting range. We saw the ancient Byzantine port of Kyrenia farther to the east, bordered by Kyrenia Castle. We took in the view and appreciated the experience of an afternoon hike among ancient ruins on a Greek island and the good time with friends and families, exploring new worlds.

We have taken you to the top of St. Hilarion to give you some perspective on our love for conversation. We could just as easily have taken you elsewhere. We've been lucky enough to have had the opportunity to travel much of the world, but our point is not that you must travel to exotic places. That just happens to be something we've done, at least at the beginning, because it was an element of the careers we chose.

We just want to establish this perspective from the start. We want to make clear that our love for conversation does not mean we reject the life of action and activity. Conversation is just one part of life—but it is an important one. And sadly, its role in the world appears to be dwindling.

Of course, when we reached the top of the castle, we had a conversation:

Bill: Hey, the sign here says Hilarion Castle was used as the model for the Cinderella castle at Disneyland.
Thomas: That's what you take away from a monument to the millennia of East Mediterranean history? Fucking Mickey Mouse? Really! You Americans.
Bill: Don't knock it. It's popular culture. If the curators think it's worth mentioning and it grabs the attention of kids, that's a good thing. And yes, this place does look like the Disney castle.

Thomas: If it was true, maybe, but it's crap for kids. The notice looks like it was scrawled by a ten-year-old. Hilarion looks nothing remotely like the Disney kitsch, which is a copy of a real Bavarian castle in Germany—Neuschwanstein Castle, if I recall from taking my daughter to Disney.

Bill: I think I prefer to believe the museum sign here, rather than your old tales.

Thomas: What I find most disturbing is that in six months' time, the only thing you'll remember about Hilarion Castle's history is the assertion that it was used to model a piece of fantasy American plastic shit. Even though it wasn't.

And so on. See, it's called conversation. (And yes, when Thomas isn't in the room, Bill continues to tell the tale of the Disney castle that is a must-see when visiting Cyprus.)

BILL: THE DAD'S TALE

Conversations can go unnoticed, but it does not mean they are forgotten or didn't have an impact.

I remember the scene quite well. On the second floor of our house in the Potomac Hills neighborhood just off Kirby Road in suburban Washington, D.C., to the right of the staircase were our bedrooms; to the left, the dining room and the living room. The kitchen was behind the dining room, and it opened up to a small backyard—the home was on a small hill, so the second floor also could open up to a backyard, as well as a second-floor porch. It was early evening. Dusk. I can't see myself—not because of the darkness but because my form has been erased from my memory. Yet I can feel my presence as I walk into the living room. I don't think I'm more than ten or eleven years old. And I don't know what has specifically precipitated the conversation with my father, who is sitting on the couch. I actually can't even see him now. My memory is of the room and the conversation.

I vaguely remember similar moments of existential angst as a child. Yes, big words for a child, *existential angst*, and, of course, those were not my words then. I only learned such terms later. But the terms really don't matter, or they only really matter when linked to the feelings and the state of mind they describe: Who am I? What am I doing? Where am I? Fear of the future, of the present, of what will be tomorrow and beyond; struggling to understand who you are and your place, not in anything as big as "the world" but simply your place.

I had been carrying this "angst" around since an incident happened at the beach in Wildwood, New Jersey, where we went almost every summer in my youth. One day as we walked back from the beach, police cars were parked by the boardwalk, and a crowd of curious bystanders had gathered, most in bathing suits, trying to get a look at what was going on. Being just a little kid, I found it easy to push my way through the crowd. I watched as the police pulled along a guy and a girl no older than their twenties, also in bathing suits but looking completely disheveled. They could barely stand up; they swayed heavily and walked so slowly, the policemen had to guide them forward. They were completely messes in their appearance. I caught a good look at their tired, old-looking faces ("old," it struck me, mainly in that these were not faces you would have expected of people their age) and their bloodshot eyes. I heard the whispering around me: "drug addicts," "stoned out of their minds," "bums." They weren't getting much sympathy from this crowd. The couple were handcuffed and put in the back of the patrol car. I watched silently. And as the crowd cleared, and life at the beach went back to its normal, easy-going, fun-loving activities, I was left stuck in my own thoughts: What had happened? How could people fall into such a state? Why was it not me there? What will prevent me from ending up as they did? Why am I headed to our beach house and them to jail? These were troubling thoughts, especially for a youngster. As we all grow older, we can at least feign answers to some of these questions. But as kids, we are just left facing a great abyss of uncertainty and fear. Will I, too, end up that way? Why not me?

So, that early evening in our living room in Potomac Hills, I sought comfort from my father from my existential angst, which must have been building within me for some time. For now, it was death itself that I, just a young boy, in good health, living a good life in suburban Washington, D.C., in the 1970s, had become preoccupied with: a crushing fear of death. Let's be clear—I wasn't worrying over my parents possibly dying or my brother or sister or friend or anyone else, for that matter. I was worried, actually deeply troubled and scared, about my own death—not a fun thing for a little boy to have on his mind. Who knows where such a morbid state of mind might lead?

We spoke. My father was and is a practical man. He'd barely finished university, preferring partying to studying. He has always been what would be called the "eternal optimist." Such morbid thoughts as worrying about one's death have always seemed the furthest thing from his mind. Even in his old age, when for the first time he began to talk about death, there was never fear in his voice, just an understanding that death was a part of life. So with my father at the time being a much younger and more naive man and me just a child, the conversation, as might be expected, was quite short. Yet there was a twist that I will remember forever. My father had showed up for this conversation with some help. He had the Old Testament in his hand. Not a worn-out one that had been read again and again. Let's just say that my family, while Jewish and knowing we were Jewish, didn't actually practice much Judaism at that time. The Old Testament he had was one of those fancy bound versions that are more for show than actual use. But again, only now do I understand what a bizarre scene it was, on so many levels, for my father. At that time in his life, he was about as secular a person as they come, yet he attempted to read to his oldest son some passages from the Old Testament, in an effort to calm some of his boy's fears. Although he surely struggled to find real meaning in those passages for himself, he still knew (instinctively?) that he could find something reassuring there to help guide me.

But in the end, my Dad decided to go with something he was more comfortable with, and old saying he would often repeat to us kids -- "Now Billy, I want you to never forget that 'there is nothing to fear but fear itself.'"

The words, the spoken words not necessarily the meaning they were trying to convey, gave me a sense of relief and peace. Maybe things weren't that bad after all. And I ran out to play kick-the-can with the other kids in the neighborhood.

Or at least that's how I'd like to remember the conversation.

It was years later that I discovered that what I thought was my Dad's line about "nothing to fear but fear itself," was actually the words of FDR at the outset of World War II. The truth did eventually sink in. Yet in the end, for me, it will always be my father who made that line famous—that evening in our living room. It was one short conversation that helped set me on course for life.

Not all conversations are actually remembered; perhaps they're even imagined. But they still can be powerful, perhaps even life changing.

05 *What's in It for Me?*

From that moment on Hugo and I fell into a conversation the like of which I have never known. We exchanged our views on art, politics, literature, religion, history, science, society, and sex. We talked without interruption all day, and often late into the night. Sometimes we laughed or shouted so much that we were asked to leave the premises.
—Iris Murdoch, *Under the Net*

WORK, PLAY, LOVE, and all the rest. Do whatever makes you an honest living and good life. But be sure to leave time—or, rather, make time—for conversation, for real conversation, with family, friends, acquaintances, even strangers. Yes, even with your kids—who may just appear uninterested, as if they're not paying attention.

What do we mean by conversation? What is this concept we are trying to hold up as so essential to humankind?

Conversation at its very essence is connection through dialogue. True conversation demands utter humility. Humility is required of both persons engaged in the conversation—one side just as much as the other. You can't be concerned about what the other will think of you. In real conversation, you also must not be concerned with getting something from the other. To be clear, however, you do want something from the other: his or her attention, interest, honest listening, and response. But that's it.

Let's be honest: Most of the time we are talking with someone in order to get something from the other person. You want a raise (in your allowance or salary); you want to get him or her into bed; you want a new client, customer, follower, or reader.

That's what we are taught, isn't it? That's what society expects of us—to engage with others to increase our capital, as Marx would look at it. Adam Smith would counter that this was the natural way of things, that we should want to connect so that our society can grow. Indeed, so the argument goes, and it is really not much different whether you are on the Left or the Right, conversation is simply a tool for interaction between humans, advancing the world and its political economy.

But that is not what we are advocating. We want conversation that leads to connection, yes, but connection without demands. I talk to you because I want to know you and want you to know me. I talk to you because I want to grow not by taking something from you, but I want to learn from you and about you. And maybe, yes, I want "something" from you but only in the sense that by talking to you and engaging with you and learning and empathizing with you, I will grow as a person.

It is a simple concept. Sound simple? Too simplistic? That's its beauty.

BILL: WILL'S TALE

Will and I had been close friends since we first met in middle school. Lots of partying together. For Will, lots of girlfriends (I was shyer and more reserved and, as a result, not a ladies' main); spring break trips to Florida; late night parties with other friends at our respective homes (depending on whose parents were away); and other typical teenage escapades.

We also talked a lot. Some of the topics were just plain gossip—I remember this particularly in middle school, still the days before cell phones, so we would spend hours talking on our phones at home. In our later teen years, the topics were heavier—often about politics (yes, we were growing up in Washington, D.C., so that, too, might be expected), as well as personal issues. There was, in fact, a small group of us who were good friends during high school (and indeed we are still friends today), and when we weren't busy with the usual stupid high school activities, like skipping school and getting drunk, we actually talked about things like religion and politics as if they really mattered to us.

We were lucky because our parents also put up with this and even encouraged us to speak up. Charlie's dad was a diplomat, and he and Charlie's mother engaged us in heated discussions—often over dinner at their home—about politics and international affairs. Jon's parents also encouraged our conversations in many ways. Jon's mom, Betsey, was a born-again Christian. She would often press me and our other friends into discussions about God and religion, not afraid to challenge us but always in a way that was accepting of our different views. Yes, we were lucky. I think we only are now beginning to realize it.

It was toward the end of our senior year. Will already knew where he'd be going to college. I was still struggling to figure out what I wanted to do and hadn't gotten into any schools I really wanted to attend. In the background of all the fun we were having in our senior year, we also had the sense that things were about to change big time for our group of tight-knit friends, each heading out on his own.

Will and I both drove to school. We had parked near each other just off Wisconsin Avenue. "Things seem to be moving so fast now. School's almost done. Where is it all leading? You ever think about it? We're going to grow old and look back, and it will all just have been a waste of time. We'll discover it was all for nothing." So, why were two high school kids talking about stuff like this at any time, but in particular just outside school on their way home? I have no idea. It seems bizarre, but that makes it no less real. The need to talk, to be heard. The feeling—not a feeling because it was simply the reality of the situation—that there was someone to talk to and confide in and get feedback from. It was not premeditated. I hadn't been brooding all day about the issue and waiting for the moment to talk about it. The thoughts just popped into my mind at the moment, and the relationship was already in place with Will and the others in our group, so it was okay to talk about anything that occurred to me.

I remember Will reassuring me. "You know, Bill, I think when we're old, we'll have all of these great memories, and that is going to be enough. That is what will keep us happy."

Years later, I mentioned this conversation to Will. He had no memory of it.

Conversations live with us—sometimes remembered, most of the time forgotten, but always there.

* * * * * *

You don't have to be rich or educated or white or black or Russian or Canadian or whatever. Everyone can partake. It's not easy, though. Our lives are rushed. We are busy. We don't have time. And when we do, others may not have time for us.

So, should you give up? No, because the "easy" solution is actually right there in front of you. Remember that high school friend you exchange Facebook messages with a couple of times a year? That cousin you really connect with who lives a couple hundred miles away, but you always have interesting conversations with, even if it's only once or twice a year? Or that colleague from work who now feels more like a friend than a coworker?

That potential partner for real conversation is right there in front of you. Just choose.

And the fun of it is that you can choose as many partners as you want. There is no limit. It's completely up to you. We are advocating for real conversation. For some people, this may be with that one good friend they've had a lifetime of real conversations with; for others, it may be with a handful of good friends; while still others might have the ability to make many people open up so that their lives are filled with endless conversations.

There is no fixed prescription for the number of conversations to pursue. All that is fixed is the basic requirement of honesty and openness that allows you to take part in really meaningful connections with others.

* * * * * *

Thomas: You want to be meaningful? We need to consider the meaning of conversation, but we should perhaps first discuss the meaning of *meaning.* This is one rock on which many of the conversations we describe have foundered, the other being the fatuous comment of Socrates at his trial that "the unexamined life is not worth living." (Unlike, no doubt, the examined death he was about to face.) Conversations, like life, are ultimately meaningless because, despite human hubris that posits otherwise, the universe itself is meaningless.

Bill: Not really sure where to begin. I thought I had succeeded in helping you escape your depressing thesis that "all is meaningless." Go ahead. What are you saying?

Thomas: The meaning of meaninglessness—or rather how to deal with it—was tackled by Albert Camus. When France was invaded by the Nazis, this philosopher, creative artist, and resistance fighter became fused into a single person, as both Camus and his Irish friend Samuel Beckett joined the dangerous underground Resistance. This is the context in which Camus wrote *The Myth of Sisyphus* in 1942. The book asked how should we confront the Absurd. "The Absurd" was a technical term Camus used in his writing. It refers to the contradiction between humanity's desire to find meaning in the universe, and the universe itself, which is completely meaningless. Once you realize that life is pointless, but you are compelled to find a point to it anyway, Camus said there are, I think, seven possible responses.

(He pauses and searches for a file on his smartphone. He finds the notes he was referring to and reads out Camus's responses to life's pointlessness.)

1. Kill yourself.
2. Ignore it by filling your life with Epicurean pleasures: food, drink, and company.
3. Live in denial. For example, become religious and say there is meaning in life because it comes from "God." Alternatively, be an existentialist and say you don't accept organized religion, but in some sense you create your own contrived "meaning of life." Camus saw both of those as forms of denial—you are not really looking life in the face because, ultimately, the universe is meaningless. (That's why he objected to being called an existentialist.)
4. Become an actor to confront the absurdities as theater. Live a life that pretends to have meaning within the context of fictions.
5. Become some other artist who creates works of art that have meaning. They will substitute for living life with meaning.
6. Become political, someone for whom power and government and the right way to use those tools fill up your time and give it an aura of meaning.

All of the above methods, Camus considered and rejected. But the final method of confronting the Absurd was the one that he actually recommended.

7.   Acceptance. Just accept that life is pointless, but that you are innately compelled by evolved human nature to find a point to it anyway. This acceptance cannot be a sad, passive, depressing state. Camus saw it as an act of resistance against the universe itself. You look at life square in the face, you don't deny it, you don't distract yourself, and you don't give in. You live anyway in the full knowledge of its pointlessness.

(Thomas looks up from his phone and continues impromptu.)

In Greek mythology, Sisyphus was doomed to roll a rock up a mountain every day and then watch it roll back down again every night. Forever! Camus said the only way Sisyphus could really be happy was if he accepted the pointlessness of his task, and he decided to own it and head down the mountain every night with a smile on his face. Living in Nazi-occupied France, being in the Resistance, formed Camus's attitude. Fighting what looked like an unwinnable battle against powerful forces engaged in pointless, inhuman destruction—that was Camus's day-to-day feeling.

The final line of his book is: "One must imagine Sisyphus happy."

Bill: But Sisyphus didn't choose to spend eternity pushing that massive stone up the hill again and again. That was his punishment.

Thomas: We were born—that's ours. We didn't choose it either.
Bill: The point of the story isn't what Camus is saying—that Sisyphus should be content with his fate. Have we forgotten why Sisyphus ended up this way? This was his punishment for his evil, deceitful ways—not something for him to be happy about. No, life is not meaningless. Life is full of meaning. That is what makes it so wonderful.

* * * * * *

What exactly are we talking about (pun intended)? What do we mean when we speak of "conversation" and the importance of conversation? If we really think that conversation is so important, there is no getting around explaining exactly what we mean.

So let's list some basic traits or characteristics of real conversation, not necessarily in any particular order.

REAL CONVERSATION IS . . .

Intimate. Do you have to be in love to have a real conversation? That, of course, depends on your definition of love. But the point should already be clear from what we've been saying until now. You can only have a real conversation with someone you feel a bond with that is not based on mutual material interests; the bond is with someone you care for because of who he or she is as a person, not because of any gain you get from engaging with the individual. Except, of course, for the "gain" that is the essence of what makes conversation so important, for everything that it does for all those engaged in true conversation.

Honest. It's a scary thing to consider. Or, at least, worrying. How honest are we in what we say? Indeed, aren't we taught not to be completely honest? This is especially so in our overly sensitive world today. You have to be so careful not only in what you do, but also in what you say. Now consider those instances when you can drop all of these concerns about being misunderstood or saying something that will get in the way of you getting what you want—when you can speak honestly with no concern about the outcome because you don't care about the outcome. What matters is just that: being completely honest and being spoken to completely honestly. That's real conversation.

Open. This is one of the best things about conversation. When you are speaking with someone in order to get something from him or her, you can never truly be open and honest with the person. You are trying to hide something about yourself, perhaps, or your motives, and are being careful to drive the conversation in a certain direction. When you can be open and honest, you can truly be free. Now, there is certainly a chicken-or-egg question with this and many of the characteristics we have listed here. When you are engaging in true conversation over time, characteristics such as openness, honesty, intimacy, and others develop. Do you first need to have openness, honesty, and so on, in your relationship with another before you can have true conversation? Or do these things come as a result of conversation? Perhaps both are possible. We have certainly experienced an immediate connection with someone whom we perhaps never met before or only barely know, and almost immediately we were able open a true dialogue. With others, it takes time.

Educational. This is not just a side benefit. It's an essential element. We aren't referring to the term *educational* in the sense of all the learning that went on in the Elysium as Socrates was in dialogue with his pupils. We will speak in more detail later about Socrates. For now, it suffices to say that those were not conversations between equals but rather a format for the learned Socrates to pass on his wisdom to his followers. Theirs was a teacher-pupil relationship, of an incredible kind. But Socrates was teaching, primarily. He was not engaged in the type of intimate conversation we are describing. That said, we do learn, expand our horizons, and even open ourselves up to new experiences in the course of real conversations. That person we are speaking with, whoever he or she may be, can show us so much, and we have so much we can offer, if only we open ourselves up to a true conversation.

And while we have distanced ourselves somewhat from the dialogues of Socrates, which might seem like the most natural place to point to an "educational" significance of true conversation, there is another great philosopher-educator who in fact might provide a better example for what we are advocating: Paulo Freire, the Brazilian activist forced into exile for his revolutionary thinking at a time when his country was under military dictatorship. The generals were correct to be scared. Freire was calling for the truest of revolutions, and he was not afraid to rip into both the fascist Right-leaning powers of political and economic oppression, as well as the reactionary so-called revolutionaries, particularly on the Left, whom he saw as wolves in sheep's clothing—that is, themselves becoming future oppressors. In *Pedagogy of the Oppressed*, Freire advocates tearing down the traditional teacher-pupil relationship, in which the latter is simply the repository of the former's so-called expertise, and replacing it with a partnership between teacher and pupil centered on dialogue. What is so beautiful about Freire's call for meaningful conversation is that it is both down to earth in the practical advice it provides to teachers and administrators (roles in which Freire himself actively participated) and visionary in recognizing the transformation it could bring to our world if only we had the courage.

What an incredible formula: education through conversation and openness results in true transformation.

Only through communication can human life have meaning. The teacher's thinking is authenticated only by the authenticity of the students' thinking. The teacher cannot think for her students, nor can she impose her thought on them. Authentic thinking does not take place in ivory tower isolation, but only in communication.[17]

(We are going to speak more later about Freire—and conversation and dialogue tools of revolution. Freire was not just an educator. He was also a revolutionary.)

Meaningful. Viktor Frankl, in *Man's Search for Meaning*, eloquently and powerfully explains how the importance of meaning to our lives. Meaning here is also taken to be purpose, the purpose for which we live. It needn't be something grand. But it must be important for the individual, and give him or her a purpose in life. Frankl built an entire philosophy from perhaps the most brutal, evil, and potentially "meaningless" abyss that humankind has fallen into, World War II Nazi extermination camps. His fate depended on whether a concentration camp

---

[17] Ibid., p. 58.

guard decided to shoot him on a whim or put him in the line to the gas chamber, things that he had little, if any, control over. From such depths, he drew the understanding that being human, remaining alive—that is, literally staying alive, but beyond that, survival—also depended on your having something meaningful for which to live.

Man's search for meaning is the primary motivation in his life and not a "secondary rationalization" of instinctual drives, according to Frankl. "This meaning is unique and specific to each individual, in that it must and can be fulfilled by him or her alone. Only then does it achieve a significance that will satisfy the will to meaning. There are some authors who contend that meanings and values are 'nothing but defense mechanisms, reaction formations and sublimations.' But as for myself, I would not be willing to live merely for the sake of my 'defense mechanisms,' nor would I be ready to die merely for the sake of my 'reaction formations.' Man, however, is able to live and even to die for the sake of his ideals and values."[18]

Yes, we need bread and water, but we also need meaning, in the sense of purpose—most importantly, purpose beyond just the will to survive. In Frankl's view, that alone—the survival instinct within us all—isn't what will keep us alive. And it certainly won't keep us happy. Here is where conversation comes in. It is through honestly speaking and listening that we discover so much, including so much about ourselves. Real Conversation helps strip away our masks, allowing us to speak truthfully and honestly; hearing about what others think of us, about who we are, what we do, and what we think, in an

---

[18] Viktor E. Frankl, The Will to Meaning (1962)

uncensored, straightforward. This is a key to our discovering and nurturing the purpose and meaning in our lives.

Uplifting. Consider for a moment before you accuse us of getting carried away. Have you never finished a conversation and felt better, even much better? Maybe it was just you doing all of the talking, as you spilled your broken heart to your best friend after your girlfriend left you. Or maybe your friend actually said things that helped you better understand how you felt and how to cope. Perhaps you had a really tough career decision to make, were struggling to figure out what to do, and then talked it through with someone you really trusted, until the way forward gradually became clear. Now that felt better, right?

Life is not easy. Where could we even begin when describing the pressures and hardships of life? Rare are the breaks. Too rare. There just isn't time. Isn't that the problem? There just isn't time for things like real conversation. Try this (and we have tried it a bunch of times because we are lucky enough to spend time in both locations): Sit down at a nice place for lunch in midtown Manhattan, a place frequented by lawyers, bankers, and other professionals, and just watch. Even at the nicest places with great food and atmosphere, people are in and out in an hour, at most. Midtown restaurants know what they are up against, so the first course is on your table minutes after you've placed your order. And these days, little, if any, alcohol is served at lunch. There is no real time to relax. At best, you can talk a little business. Now, to continue our experiment, join us for lunch in Nicosia. Wine or beer is a must, even at lunch. And the pace—well, if you finished the meal in less than an hour, you'd leave embarrassed that you'd said something wrong. They say we live in small world, but luckily, the American way of life has not completely taken over—in particular, in the eastern Mediterranean. And with the slower pace comes the opportunity to relax a little, to give your mind (and the conversation) a break from the usual gruel. And then throw in a glass or two of Vasilikon (you actually can't go wrong with either the red or the white). Now, doesn't that feel good? And by the way, doesn't that leave us some time to digress a bit from the normal boring banter? We are just back from a short trip to Athens, and it never ceases to amaze us that despite the economic mess there—massive unemployment; wages slashed; pensions slashed; economy in a shambles, despite all efforts to turn things around—the coffee shops and the restaurants just off Syntagma Square are all hopping. To say nothing about the more upper-class neighborhood of Kaloniki where, despite the numerous restaurants and coffee shops lining the streets and promenades, it can be hard to find a seat. The conversations abound and are at times noisy but beautifully noisy.

Communicative. Conversation, dialogue, speaking, and inter-acting are ultimately about communication. But not just any communication. I can ask you to explain something or to do me a favor or even argue with you about something, but that does not, in and of itself, mean we are having a real conversation. The type of communication we are referring to involves opening oneself up to the other—to both give her your full attention and to be open up to her input. To talk about what you really care about and listen, knowing that you are hearing things of real interest and concern to the person with whom you are speaking.

Connective. Real conversation is not just about talking. There must also be connection, empathy, and concern. Real conversation involves encounter. There must be a real meeting of the minds and of emotions.

No one—no couple, friends, colleagues, lovers, or family members—no one is capable or would even want to always or even most of the time be engaged in the type of conversation we are describing. It is an ideal—an ideal that can be achieved but only in passing, yet still significant, instances.

06   *The Ultimate Connection?*

*Not a sentence or a word is independent of
the circumstances under which it is uttered.*
—Alfred North Whitehead

W E ENTER CONVERSATIONS in order to convince. We have
our opinion. We hold it to be the Truth. We speak to others
in order to persuade them to accept our Truth. This is not
true conversation, not true dialogue, but the "hostile, polemical
argument." Or alternatively, we become frustrated and angered
by "the other" who does not hold to our Truths, and we simply
stop speaking with them and only engage with others who are
like us. This is a recipe for failed conversation. Neither party
is challenged. Neither is questioning the other. In sameness
comes complacency and dullness.

Freire, the late Brazilian educator we quote extensively
here, has only one demand of those who take part in true
dialogue: love.

> Dialogue cannot exist, however, in the
> absence of a profound love for the world

and for people. Love is at the same time the foundation of dialogue and dialogue itself. It is thus necessarily the task of responsible Subjects and cannot exist in a relation of domination. Domination reveals the pathology of love: sadism in the dominator and masochism in the dominated. Because love is an act of courage, not of fear, love is commitment to others. No matter where the oppressed are found, the act of love is commitment to their cause—the cause of liberation. And this commitment, because it is loving, is dialogical. As an act of bravery, love cannot be sentimental; as an act of freedom, it must not serve as a pretext for manipulation. It must generate other acts of freedom; otherwise, it is not love. Only by abolishing the situation of oppression is it possible to restore the love which that situation made impossible. If I do not love the world—if I do not love life—if I do not love people—I cannot enter dialogue.[19]

We forgive you, Paulo Freire. We understand you are a revolutionary at heart. Education was your means; radical change, your goal. Radical change would mean real freedom—not just freedom to earn a fair wage (and Freire was critically aware that he would be attacked for having his head in the

---

[19] Ibid., pp. 70–71.

clouds and not being concerned with putting food on the table for the underprivileged)—but freedom to think unrestrained. Freire, you were brilliant because you recognized that freedom is not something you put in place from above, with new laws and new government. Freedom is established from the ground up. It takes a revolution in our educational systems to bring about a true revolution. We forgive you, Paulo Freire, for being so political—because whether someone agrees or disagrees with your political aims, your underlying humanity is an example for us all.

"If I do not love the world—if I do not love life—if I do not love people—I cannot enter dialogue."

It sounds petty. So simplistic. Maybe even a little pathetic. All this talk of love. Shouldn't this just be dismissed as Left Wing drivel, 1960s flower children talk long past its day? "All you need is love" makes for a great song, but beyond that, what's the value?

Perhaps it's best to tone it down a little. How about "common ground" as the basis of true conversation—isn't that a fair and realistic idea?

BILL: THE LOVERS' TALE

We were sitting on the sidewalk in the middle of town. Yet that must be a trick of my memory. We would have been walked over and yelled at. So I probably have that wrong. But everything else I remember vividly. Not the exact words but definitely the content—and the feelings that went with the words. I was scared and mixed-up and nervous, all wrapped in one. What the hell was I doing? What the hell was I thinking about?

It wasn't at all fair what I was asking. How could I expect him to take responsibility for my life's decisions? This was really just up to me, but that didn't stop me from talking about it. My wedding was set for the next day. Family and friends had flown from all over to join us for the occasion. And here I was, having second thoughts? Getting cold feet? My brother tried valiantly to calm my nerves. He reminded me what a fantastic, beautiful woman my future wife was. He assured me I was doing the right thing. I know now it was an unfair question I had asked my brother. I also know that it was fine to ask and that real conversations are often about things for which there are no real answers. But what I really wonder now, looking back, because I was not able to see the question at the time, is how marriage fits into the puzzle whose pieces also include conversation and all of its parts, such as connection, empathy, friendship, and caring.

Much later in life, Buber opened my eyes to the possibility— or, more correctly, put meaning and understanding behind the sense I had from my life's experiences about the importance of conversation—that it was of potentially penultimate importance. Buber seems to point to the possibility of our real conversations leading to the highest reaches we can attain as humans, something actually beyond humanity in a spiritual realm Buber is smart enough to avoid trying too hard to define. Buber reminds us that while there is a God "the all powerful" in the Old Testament, there is also God "the passionate and loving and forgiving." The former might be seen as the God of Exodus, the latter the God of the "Song of Songs":

1. Behold thou art fair, my love, behold, thou art fair,
    Thine eyes are as doves behind thy veil;
    Thy hair is a flock of goats,
    That trail down from Mount Gilead.

2. Thy teeth are like a flock of ewes all shaped alike,
    Which are come up from the washing;
    Whereof all are paired,
    And none faileth among them.

3. Thy lips are liked a thread of scarlet,
    And thy mouth is comely;
    Thy temples are like a pomegranate split open
    Behind thy veil.

4. Thy neck is like the tower of David
    Builded with turrets,
    Whereon there hang a thousand shields,
    All the armor of the mighty men.

5. Thy two breasts are like two fawns,
    That are twins of a gazelle,
    Which feed among lilies.[20]

Reams have been written about this sensual poem that not only made its way into the Jewish holy texts, but that in many synagogues today still makes up a central part of the weekly Sabbath eve services. I'm no Jewish scholar, but I can

---

[20] "The Song of Songs," Chapter 4, from *The Five Megilloth*, edited by Dr. A. Cohen (London: Soncino Press, 1946), pp. 13–14.

certainly relate to the power of this text, of its likening of the connection between two lovers to that of the highest, most beautiful potential connection between the human and the divine. (I'm less sure my wife would like to be told her hair is like a flock of goats and her teeth are like sheep.)

My brother did get me to my wedding, and I have him to thank for that, for giving me that little push I needed to take the wonderful—indeed, incredible—leap of faith that true relationship entails. He sent me on the way toward perhaps the most central conversation of my life. My wife was similarly taking a leap of faith. Did we really know each other? We had been going out for several years and lived together before deciding to get married, but opening up takes time and commitment and is not easy.

Marriage as conversation. For me, so far it has been the most beautiful conversation I have experienced and that I hold most dear.

* * * * * *

We sit over dinner and discuss a wide range of topics. But then, within that exchange, there are moments, flashes of intimacy, of honesty when we delve into ourselves and those with whom we are speaking with concern for them, for ourselves, for the community and the world around us.

"All real living is meeting."[21]

---

[21] Martin Buber, *I and Thou*, translated by Ronald Gregor Smith (Edinburgh), p. 10.

Sadly, perhaps, we normally have an ulterior motive when we enter into conversation. We want something of that person with whom we are conversing. We want him or her to give us something, maybe to help or to trick the person into helping us. Perhaps we are looking to sell the individual something. And perhaps we are bending the truth a little (or even a lot) in order to get what we want. "Of course, the car is in great shape," you say, knowing full well the main reason you are selling it is that for the umpteenth time this year, you just got the car out of the mechanic's shop last week and promised yourself finally to get rid of it. Now, that probably isn't the first thing you are going to say to the guy who answers the "for sale" advertisement. You might not even mention that fact at all. Maybe you'll even throw in "The car drives great" and leave out "when it isn't broken down and in the shop."

But don't get us wrong. Conversations whose aim is to "get something"—and, clearly, this is what most conversations are about—don't always have evil ulterior motives. Maybe you are trying to raise money for a good cause or doing something as simple as asking a neighbor for a couple of eggs because you've run out or to pick up your kids from football practice because you need to be somewhere.

But no matter how well or poorly intentioned, these conversations, the interactions we have with friends and family and even strangers, are such that the "other" we are communicating with is simply a means for us to employ to our advantage (even when the aim is to do something good).

There may even be a common purpose. The goal of the discourse is for the good of both parties. But the dialogue still never rises beyond that of I and You. We remain objects, mere tools, whether for a common or conflicting purpose. Indeed, most conversation is stuck at "I and It." We see the other as an object, to be interacted with for our benefit.

The conversation we are advocating is of a different category. Perhaps we will go so far as to say it falls under the I-Thou relationship. You can accept the spiritual significance or not. It doesn't really matter.

The recognition of the sublime power of conversation—of the emotional and, yes, spiritual space that we can define for ourselves, which is so badly needed in our ever-demanding, degenerating material world, through real conversation—can be purely human in nature. There is no demand for a god. Perhaps real conversation itself can be seen as one of the pillars of a secular godhead of the truly enlightened human—stripped of both the material and so-called spiritual (i.e. ., religious) constructs that hide her from herself.

Together, we see through the facades. Together, we slowly begin to understand who we really are, what is really important, what it means to be truly ourselves and what great potential it entails.

It is intimate and uplifting and completely honest.

* * * * * *

We sit outside around two large tables laid out awkwardly, as old tables and chairs can be that are brought together by need and not design. The smell from the lamb grilling on the barbecue is mouth watering. Tantalizing dish after dish of traditional Greek food is brought out from the old stone barn that our good Cypriot friend had built into a small home in the hilltop village. The sun has set. To one side you can still make out the Mediterranean and to the other, the Troodos

Mountains. It was not long before the red wine was flowing. "Yamas!"

Yes, the great wine. We had stopped by the nearby family-owned Vasilikon winery earlier in the day on our way to Terra. Georgios met us just outside the new building that now housed the winery. What a change! It was just over a decade ago when our friend first introduced us to Georgios Kyriakides and his brother Giannis. At the time, you really couldn't yet describe them as winery owners. In those days, we would stop by the wooden construct, small and with the look of a large shed or a small barn, on a corner of the family farm just outside Kathikas. The village was a windy thirty-minute drive from the seaside town of Paphos. Georgios and Gianni greeted us warmly and were also quick to run back into the small storeroom and bring out a bottle or two for us to taste. It was on one of our first visits that they told us their story: The brothers had left the family farm to seek opportunities in America, as they and their entire family saw it at the time. The village was not the right place for smart, hardworking men in their twenties who were looking to make money and something of their lives. America was the land of opportunity, so off they went. As Georgios and Gianni tell it, things went well in America. They succeeded, if success is measured in terms of a good job and an opportunity to grow professionally. But after a few years, they grew homesick for their family, for the warm Mediterranean climate, and for the slower, simpler way of life they had grown up with in a small village in a relatively remote corner of this Greek island.

But what to do back in Kathikas? The family farm could barely support their parents.

Then they had an idea: plant their own vineyards, and purchase grapes from area farmers already growing them, and start producing wine.

Their idea worked. First, the customers were people like us who lived in nearby villages or were visiting friends there. And the Kyriakides brothers largely made the wine and sold the wine themselves from their small hut on the corner of the family farm.

But as the worldwide wine craze also hit Cyprus (on one of our visits Georgios excitedly told us how several Chinese importers had just visited him and placed a major order), the brothers' story turned Hollywood-ish. Not only had they successfully returned home to their small Cyprus village, but they had also made it big. No more working out of the barn. They were able to build a two-story winery with a massive porch overlooking the family vineyards on the hilltop and the not-too-far-distant Mediterranean below. There, they received visitors for wine tasting,

So that June afternoon, as we had done many times before, we picked up a case of Vasilikon and from there headed to Terra.

We had a small change in plans when, after a walk around the village and dinner preparations, our Cypriot friend brought out a bottle of Zivania. In all honesty, it was not one of our favorite drinks, but who could say no to a few toasts? So we sat underneath an old fig tree and took in the fresh air and magnificent view, as we awaited the arrival of a few other friends and neighbors.

There was really not much that needed to be said at that moment. The great food and conversation would begin later.

"In the beginning is relation."[22]

Conversation evades us, even though we are provided with infinite opportunities to engage in real conversation. It is present in both words and actions. It is dialogue at its simplest level, but it is also most basically an encounter. The conversations in our lives can include simple glances, as well as long talks. Words and actions weave together. They awaken and inspire us. Our eyes are opened, as are our souls. We grow. We are enlightened. We enter a realm that is just waiting for us, patiently, although we at best hesitate and more often simply ignore it. We have become conditioned to live our lives with the minimal amount of engagement. Opening up to real conversation involves risks. To engage with the Other is to risk rejection, even potential humiliation. It is to put your ideas and beliefs to the test. For most people, that is not a risk they want to take. Most arrive at the moment of encounter with their guard up so high, there is no chance for real connection. You must be confident to succeed with conversation. You must be confident enough to be shown you are wrong, to be taken on a new path you never encountered before or even rejected in the past. You must have an open mind, curious to explore and discover.

But we are getting ahead of ourselves and in so doing giving the wrong impression. There are no prerequisites for Real Conversation. It is not just for certain types of people with certain characteristics.

Real conversation, an honest engagement with the Other in words and action, is both a phenomenon and a process. As

---

[22] Ibid., p. 17.

phenomenon, it is a single instance of honesty and openness while engaging with someone. It actually requires nothing, if you accept the premise that all humans have the capacity for open and honest engagement. Sadly, life may stamp out this tendency; it may suppress it. Yet it remains within all humans, revealing itself from time to time just briefly but always there in the background. Real conversation as process, as something a person consciously guides herself toward, strengthens the tendency toward honesty and openness. The more a person engages in real conversation, the more it becomes second nature.

There is nothing conscious about real conversation at the start, nor does there need to be ever.

* * * * * *

We met on the job, as often happens, despite coming from very different backgrounds and upbringing. It was a noisy newsroom in the days just before the Internet arrived and things in newsrooms were done the old-fashioned way: There were no emails or WhatsApp groups to communicate with. If you wanted a colleague's attention, you had to shout across the newsroom. There was no spell-check on the computer or Wikipedia. So unless you wanted to waste time on your deadline trying to track down an encyclopedia or a dictionary, you were constantly calling out to this or that colleague whom you thought might have the answer you needed. On top of all the chatter between colleagues at work, there was the loud, demanding shouting of an editor pissed off about one thing or demanding something else. The shouts intensified as the night rolled on and the deadline neared. Those were also the days when people were still dumb enough not only to smoke but to smoke in offices. So you get the picture: a smoky, noisy newsroom. One of us was a veteran world-traveled journalist turned editor. The other was barely out of college and at his first newspaper job. Neither of us can put our finger on just where our conversation started in that busy newsroom. Maybe it didn't even happen there but instead at the bar we both frequented after work in a neighborhood where, by chance, one of us had a girlfriend and the other a good friend. An encounter so profound that we can't remember it? A talk that has been going for over three decades, with the details long forgotten? What kind of advocates for conversation can we be with such a history? We're the kind who understand that the essence of real conversation is not in the particulars of any one of an infinite number of dialogues we had together, but in the deep realization of the importance of the encounters—always invigorating, eye-opening, and challenging. Not by conscious choice. Not by design. Not with any goal in mind. But simply by coming to the table with an open mind, an eagerness to listen, speak, and connect and in this way to grow as a person.

07 *Thirty Years and Counting*

I heard myself boasting, lying, exaggerating.
Oh, not deliberately, far from it.
It would be unconvivial and dull to
stop the flow of talk and speak
only after carefully considering
whether I was telling the truth.
                                        —Bernard Berenson

WRITING IS IN our blood. We love it. Yes, sometimes it doesn't come easy. And at those times it can even be painful, almost literally. You are already minutes past deadline, and you have the night editor screaming at you to get the story done already. Yet you just can't get out that perfect lead, and you know without it the story will be lost.

So you struggle. And sometimes it works, and sometimes it doesn't.

Writing is a profession, a trade. Perhaps now a fast-disappearing trade.

Just look at the crap posted online. Or the lousy writing we see from candidates for posts we are trying to fill. Even young people out of the best colleges and universities don't always know how to write well.

We were lucky, in a way. We learned to write not just in school but at work. We wouldn't have lasted long in a newsroom if we hadn't honed our skills to the point where we could sit down an hour before deadline and pump out a clearly written story. No bullshit. No fancy terminology. No corporate crap with lots of big words but little on clarity. Just clear English explaining the who, what, why, and how of the story.

There's probably no better way to learn how to write.

There's not much room at a wire service or a good international newspaper for the type of creative writing that blurs the message in poetic and literary playfulness. That may result in great novels but isn't supposed to be the style of a seasoned journalist.

Why are we telling you all of this? Because that is where we first met —in a newsroom thirty years ago—and first started talking.

We'd like to think that our conversation was like that of any two people who are on the way to becoming good friends: easygoing, enjoyable, interesting, and engaging.

But before we talk more about our conversation, we'll mention one other point connected to our backgrounds in journalism. At least in our day, if you didn't know how to ask questions and listen carefully to the answers (and do this while taking notes, sometimes for hours on end in multiple interviews—not in fancy air-conditioned offices but in the field—and thinking of follow-up questions and observing what was happening around you and how all of this connected to the story you were trying to write), you wouldn't go far as a journalist.

No, a journalistic interview is not a conversation. At least, it isn't necessarily one.

Yet a good one can have some of the same traits. The journalist must be good listener, paying attention to what is being said, how it is being said, and in what context. He or she must demonstrate real empathy. You won't get far in an interview or in a conversation without showing empathy to the person you are speaking to. The dialogue will go nowhere if don't connect to the person with whom you are speaking. We are, of course, talking about an in-depth interview—not just when a couple of questions are being thrown, for instance, at a politician running to her next meeting. The interviewee must trust you. If she thinks you aren't going to get her story right, she won't fully cooperate in the interview.

This all applies even more when you're dealing with confidential sources, with whom it is necessary to not only show empathy, but also demonstrate trust and discretion. No potential confidential source is going to open up to you if he isn't convinced he can trust you. It wouldn't be worth the risk.

Now, can you fake these things—empathy, trust, discretion? Can you fake people into opening up, whether in an interview or a conversation? Of course, you can. We'd like to think that this is a route we never took, but we admit, in particular after leaving journalism and entering the world of private intelligence (which we will talk about later). As journalists, we always felt we were on the right side. As intelligence professionals, well let's just say there are instances when the lines between good and bad are blurred. And the client you are working for isn't always on the good side. Sadly, today it will sound phony to the jaded ears of many people that as journalists, we believed and were committed to only the truth—and, even more carefully, to the truth being presented not only clearly and fairly but in a manner in which the innocent would not be made to suffer, due to our work.

We wrote believing that if we told the story, it would help make the world a better place.

Shame on the cynics, both then and today, who see (and use) journalism as a tool for the powerful. They have turned the conversation on its head. Indeed, they have very nearly destroyed the conversation. It's not complicated, and it's not new. Fake news has been around as long as humans have been telling stories and hoping those stories would influence others. Spin isn't something invented by some hotshot political consultants. Spinning tales has been around as long as storytelling has, whether it be in modern newspapers and books or in ancient legends and myths. So have unscrupulous politicians and business people trying to use disinformation to advance their own aims. Journalists' job, our job when we were full-time journalists ourselves, was to cut through the crap, expose whoever was trying to spin it, and show the public the real story.

THOMAS: THE JOURNALIST'S TALE

I was enjoying the walk from the office when the man with the Kalashnikov blocked my path. Two companions, also with guns, flanked him. Their appearance was so similar, it had to be a uniform. Of course. Beirut. Everyone who was anybody has a uniform.

This one was jeans, black T-shirt, and a red bandanna around the forehead, over wild black hair. I guess the unkempt beards counted as uniform, too. The bandannas bore a single white word in Arabic, which I recognized as *Allah*. That was chilling. It identified them as Shi'ite militiamen—on a mission. The front man held his gun across his chest, blocking my path.

In one of those odd moments that embedded itself in memory, I noticed not him, but a red earth mound fifty meters behind him. It was a barricade marking someone's territory, covered in grass and weeds. There was one shrub on top, and a sparrow perched there started chirping. I laughed. Even sparrows mark their territory with a barricade in Beirut.

The man thrust his face forward. He wasn't laughing.

"What are you?" he said.

"A journalist."

"Not work." His voice rose. "What? American? French? English?"

Of course, I thought, stomach churning. Three favorite kidnap nationalities for Shi'ite militias. Man on a mission, indeed.

In Beirut, you learn to fake courage. Macho militiamen despise weakness, respect defiance. So I laughed again.

"I'm Irish," I said, with an edge that suggested annoyance at being mistaken for any one of the nationalities he suggested.

Not that it mattered. One Irish teacher had already vanished into Beirut's kidnapping black hole.

He glowered. "EERSH? What is eersh?"

"Irish!" I snapped with irritation. "Ireland. Irlande!"

He turned to consult with the other two, shaking his head. In their Arabic babble I heard "Eersh" repeated, tossed around. One of the others looked at me.

"Is Eersh eera?"

What the fuck did that mean? I scrabbled through my memory banks, looking for a match.

"Eera," he shouted and pointed his AK-47 skyward. He fired a volley. "Ee Er Ay. Bang bang!"

It clicked.

"Yes, yes," I said. "That's it. IRA!"

They babbled again, enlightenment obvious on their faces. The leader confronted me again.

"You are Era?"

"Yes, I am!"

He lowered the gun to one side, slapped me on the shoulder.

"Yah! Very good. Eera very good. Anti-imperialist. Fighters."

"Yes," I said and grasped his hand. "Very good. Warriors. Like you."

He said something to his companions, and they stepped to one side, freeing my path.

"Welcome in Beirut," he said.

"Very nice to meet you," I said, deliberately not thanking them for letting me go.

As I walked away, my shoulder blades itched, but I had tried to stop flinching at the sound of guns in Beirut. A volley chattered into the air behind me. If you could hear it, you were okay.

I turned, punched my fist into the air, and they did the same. As I passed the barricade, the sparrow started chirping again.

"Fucking right," I said. "Saved from Beirut terrorists by Irish terrorists. God is great!"

08 Write It Down; or Perhaps Don't

The real art of conversation is not only
to say the right thing in the right place
but to leave unsaid the wrong
thing at the tempting moment.
—Dorothy Nevill

WHERE DO YOU begin the conversation today if you can't even agree on the basic facts of the story—the who, what, when, where, and why? In today's environment, the conversation is always dangerously close to being—if not in fact—stillborn. And while the metaphor of the stillborn conversation is a gross exaggeration in so many ways, it is also meant as a wake-up call. What lives when there is no longer conversation? What is life when there is no longer true and open dialogue? And where do we all end up; where does our world end up?

Your authors began their real conversation after work, which was in the late hours of the night. We were young and single, so in no rush to get home and happy to head to a nearby bar. The conversations were often very heated. We'd like to think that this was because we really cared about the topics we discussed and argued about. But we admit that there was also a lot of ego involved—the big egos of journalists who think that they have the real inside look and insight about what is going on in the world and that their opinions really matter, at least much more than the average person's.

Who were we kidding, and who are we still kidding? Did Thomas and Bill really have something important to say in all of those years? Wasn't it all just utter bullshit? Babble that just helped pass the time in our simple, pathetic lives? Who are we to think we actually came to some important conclusions, that we actually in our discussions came to a better understanding of anything?

We must admit, when we set out to write this book our first thought was to sit down across a table with a tape recorder between us and start talking. We actually tried it a few times. And yes, it was a complete flop. There were few, if any, words of wisdom. Most of it was boring drivel. We'd like to think that in those two or three sessions, we weren't at our best. We certainly weren't our natural selves, with the tape recorder staring at us when normally all we had between us was a bottle of scotch or wine. And there was, of course, no way to recreate the experience and atmosphere that developed between us during those three decades of talking.

We should have taken a lesson we learned a few years ago from a friend, Joe Healy—one of the most renowned insurance investigators in the United States who passed away several years ago, but only after he had a chance to put some of his great tales into a book. You see, Joe was the consummate storyteller, and decades of working on some of the most complex (and gory and bizarre) death and injury claims during those years had given him lots of great material.

Joe was a true gentleman. When we asked him whether he could help our company expand its complex insurance fraud investigations unit, he jumped on board immediately. He would come down to our office in Washington, D.C., or we'd meet him up at his home in New Jersey. He knew all the key people in the insurance claims industry, and no one knew better than him how to run an investigation into a suspicious claim. He was a tremendous person to work with. He knew so much and shared his expertise in a manner that we can certainly say, even now, years later, that everything we know of any importance about this sector came from Joe.

During our meetings, it was all business. But afterward, often over a long lunch or drinks after work, with just a little egging on, Joe would tell us about one of his more interesting cases—from plane crashes and faked accidents and deaths to how a criminal and even a terror group uses insurance fraud to raise funds.

The stories were great and Joe's ability to tell them, even better. He delivered every twist and punch with ease and accuracy.

But when he tried to put it all down in a book—well, it just didn't work. There just wasn't the same flow and cadence as when he actually told the stories himself, in person.

So, if one of the best of storytellers couldn't pull it off, we suppose we shouldn't feel too bad about ourselves not being able to simply start talking to each other and in that matter create a book of conversations. Playwrights and screenwriters struggle with dialogue, so it's probably okay that we did, too.

We've engaged in thirty years of conversation as friends and colleagues, and, you know, it's been incredible. There have literally been no ups and downs. It has all been good. Very good. We've explored, grown personally and intellectually, solved problems, come up with problems we haven't yet solved and maybe never will, consoled each other, laughed together, and had lots of fun all these years—and all that just talking.

We'd like to believe we've also become better people in the process. There really is no way around it. If the person with whom you are engaged in real conversation is constantly challenging you, as he or she should, to explain yourself, to explain what you believe or think or want, to the point that you feel more secure in certain of your ideas and behaviors, others you amend, and yet others you change completely, the results can only be good for you.

Silence leads nowhere. Of course, we don't mean the silence of listening, which is really not silence as you actively engage with another. The silence that leads nowhere is the silence of those who refuse to or have become unable to engage in real conversation. They are stuck—stuck with their own ideas and thoughts, unchallenged by others, and in particular by others who think differently than they do. They are stuck with themselves. How boring. Perhaps we should go as far as to say, "How pathetic."

There is also the silence in thinking. We aren't knocking this. Indeed, we are advocates. Part of the importance of turning off the phone and the computer (we will talk more about this later) and the television and the radio is to give yourself room, a quiet space, to think. We realize that some people say they think best with the radio on and music playing, so let's call it the silence of solitude, which offers an essential creative space for us to think. We are advocates. Where else to, for instance, enjoy a good book? We are both avid readers. We see what reading has meant for us—opening up new worlds and new ideas. But what good are they if we don't share them? What good are they if we don't test this newfound knowledge?

People sometimes change over time—and even more so when the time lapse covers many years. We change physically, emotionally, and ideologically. Our conversation when we were both single One was just out of university in his first job as a journalist. The other had already traveled the world, fallen in love, and been married and then divorced and was at the peak of his profession—an editor in great demand. We married and remarried. Children entered the scene. We moved on to new jobs and even new professions. And all the time, the conversation continued.

We say *conversation* and not *conversations* because true conversation is not a one-night stand or a series of them. It is a continuum whose starting point quickly becomes unimportant and an end, when it comes, that is nearly always unforeseen.

So, what have we talked about all these years? Life.

That's probably the best way to describe the essence of our conversation. Perhaps it is what needs to drive all real conversation.

We talk about the people we care about, the things we care about, the ideas we care about. We talk about our beliefs and fears. We talk about our problems. We talk about things practical—how to handle business and family issues—and things "impractical," like how to change the world and the meaning (or lack thereof) of life and death.

Maybe our next book will be a survey of *Great Ideas from Plato to Pluto.* Or an analysis of *U.S. Policy in the Eastern Mediterranean* or *Central Asia.* Yes, we actually talk about these things, and we talk about them passionately. We do this at least in part because we have been lucky enough in our own lives to have been exposed to many cultures and peoples and have seen the effects in some cases firsthand of various policies, ideologies, and business interests. We talk big. We have an admittedly inflated view of our place within these issues. (And we remind ourselves of this a lot— "Why should anyone care what we think, anyway?") But we ultimately always come down to earth: How should I live my life? What do I believe? What do I want from my life?

These are questions with no firm answers. That is what makes them so beautiful and important. You should never stop thinking about them. And while, yes, in our everyday crazily busy lives who has time for considering such things? No one, of course. But what your authors have done, and you can do also, is find a little time once a week or even once a month to slow down, and ... talk, talk about the things that are on your mind.

So, yes, we have some very strong opinions about things personal and political, about local issues and international issues. But in the context of our current discussion—about the importance of conversation in one's personal and public life— our opinions and views really don't matter. It is the conversation itself that counts. Indeed, views and beliefs often change. Conversation, when open and engaging and challenging, as it should be, provides a key platform for a person to test and develop his or her thoughts.

Your authors' views have changed over the years. We changed as a result of our experiences and as our understanding grew. Our views changed as a result of how we synthesized and internalized our experiences and understanding during our conversations.

That's one of the fun things about not having the tape recorder on (or, for that matter, exchanging ideas or arguing over WhatsApp or in Facebook postings). You can say what you want, change your mind about something, and not have anyone point a finger at you for what you believe or believed. Conversation be a free-for-all. Ours often are. There is no fear of being misunderstood because as the conversation progresses you can explain yourself, and there's no trail for you later to be attacked about. There is honesty in the moment that passes unrecorded. In our minds, of course, the memory of what was said may remain. Time will at least blur the memory and likely eventually erase it. If anything at all remains, it is the essence: the underlying meaning and feeling and belief that were expressed, if indeed they were significant enough to be noted in our minds. There is the potential of freedom in the spoken word—freedom to think and explore in ways the written word does not allow. This is not a call to anarchy or, worse, does not advocate the use of conversation—in particular, private conversation—to engage in bigoted, chauvinistic, or other vile dialogue. That is completely unacceptable and goes against everything we believe and are advocating.

Yet we still recognize, and hope others also see, that free thinking and free talking allow you to go places that the written word would never permit because of a fear of, or a concern about, being misunderstood. We hesitate here to even give examples, for fear of them being misconstrued. Perhaps it's best to take as an example a topic that, while hot and driven by strong and emotional feelings on all sides, still allows for some latitude in expression. So in our conversations, for instance, about religion, a topic on which we have strong views and experiences, we can speak openly about our atheism and our beliefs, our doubts and our struggles, without fear of judgment. We have always spoken freely with each other.

We can argue with what the other has said. We can explore an idea and see where it leads. We are even open to changing our minds about something. Let's repeat that—as we talk and reason and criticize and deconstruct and laugh and maybe even cry, our conversation becomes a vehicle for change. And if not for change, then at a minimum for insight and intellectual and emotional growth. It has been for us. It can be for you as well.

Through our thirty-year conversation, we have broadened each other's horizons. That's what real conversation does. We each brought our particular baggage to the table and opened it up and shared the contents with the other. Not in one swoop but over time. And over time in which our own baggage was losing some things and gaining others. We challenged each other. We questioned each other. We criticized each other, attempting to rip apart ideas and beliefs we took for granted. We worked out problems together, some related to personal issues and others to business ones.

The two of us are not very "open" people. We don't like talking about our feelings. Neither of us has Facebook or regularly uses any type of social media. Part of that is due to our work in private intelligence, which we've been engaged in for around twenty years now. We will discuss that in more detail in a later chapter. But for now, suffice it to say that in our line of work, you get to see a lot of the downside of having too much of a public profile.

So while we have always, and will continue here, not to talk much about ourselves, there is one personal issue that may go to the core of our advocating conversation: On the face of it (and maybe not just on the face of it), we are very different people: one, an American Jew; the other, an Irish Catholic. We're twenty years apart in age. When we started our conversation, the American one of us was just out of university in the States, with no real professional experience. The Irishman had already managed to fly Vulcan nuclear bombers for the RAF, write children's books, and open a Reuters bureau. Or so he says.

Thomas: The Birds' Tale

We expected the "boom" when we dropped our final 500-pound bomb on the training range off the island's coast. The second boom, we did not. It was closer, louder, and it shook the dark claustrophobic cabin. The four crewmen froze; four brains raced to compute an assessment. The bat-winged RAF bomber continued roaring through the sky 500 feet above the sea. John, the captain, broke the silence.

"Bird strike! We hit a griffon vulture. Both starboard engines out. Crew, advise your status!"

Operating as air electronics officer, I was now in charge. I controlled all electrical power that kept the plane flying. The engines ran four alternators that operated everything electrical and electronic. I scanned the captain's black alternator control panel, at the same time slamming upward a square switch to its left.

"Non-essentials tripped," I said. The switch shut down all systems using power, except for the flight controls, the instruments, and the radio.

Young Eric, the copilot, was droning out a Mayday call like a laundry list. "Bird strike, both port engines out, position."

"Starboard!" John shouted on the intercom. "Fucking starboard out, you idiot!" Eric's mistake raised the tension. This was no training drill; this was real.

"Correction, correction. Starboard engines out, repeat starboard only out." Eric still sounded calm but a bit louder, no longer nonchalant. Rod, the navigator, passed Eric our position. Twenty miles east of our coastal airbase, heading 098, speed 280 knots.

"Foxtrot 93, I have you on radar. Maintain altitude and heading." A steady, reassuring voice from ground control. Women controllers always sounded so much better than men in an emergency.

My alternator panel showed the two starboard power generators disconnected. On the panel, they were two short white horizontal indicators above a thick white line that represented the bomber's systems. Two other white indicators on the left were vertical, connected to the systems' line. Two alternators were good enough to fly a plane with all engines running. With the asymmetric drag of two engines out, the demand for power to the flight controls would be enormous. If one other alternator failed, it was possible that both would.

I had two backup power units, an auxiliary power pack, the AAP, and a ram air turbine—"the RAT," of course. The AAP was an extra alternator in the wing, powered by a small fuel engine. I decided to bring it online at once. I reached up to a panel on the top left and banged in a plunger. We heard a distant low whine as the engine fired. Three seconds to run up, then the backup indicator should snap onto his panel systems line.

Outside the side window, I surveyed the sea and a tilted horizon. Horizons should be straight. I glanced at the panel. The altimeter showed 300 feet; it should have been 500.

"Maintain altitude and heading," the ground controller repeated.

Eric grimaced at the captain but said nothing. If the plane wheeled over and dropped, John would order Eric to eject, so that there was a survivor. The rest of us would die—there were only two ejection seats, not four. Four seconds. I glared at the AAP indicator. Nothing.

"Captain. AAP failed to start. Release the RAT."

The RAT was a simple air-driven fan unit with a quarter of the power of an alternator. The last resort. It could deliver enough power to land a plane that was close to home, flying straight and level. John pulled a handle on his panel—a cable release that dropped the RAT down from the wing into the air flow.

On my alternator panel, a short white line flickered. It went horizontal, vertical, horizontal, dithered for two seconds, then stuck. Vertical. Attached to the systems bar, delivering power. One second later, the third main alternator failed. The scene outside again caught the corner of my eye. The horizon was, well, horizontal.

"RAT and Alternator One steady online," I said.

"Foxtrot 93 from Tower. Lower the undercarriage when ready and begin your descent. Cleared to land runway 030. ETA seven minutes."

"Roger Tower, descending." John switched to intercom.

"Captain to crew. Well done, Thomas. We're in good shape, thanks to you. Pre-landing checks, please."

From bird strike to touchdown was nine minutes. That was a short crew conversation. It seemed longer.

09

A Work in Progress

*A person isn't who they are during the
last conversation you had with them—
they're who they've been throughout
your whole relationship.*
—Rainer Maria Rilke

As friends, we're quite a mismatch. And while we do like each other, the message is not similar to a Hollywood love story in which "opposites attract." That may be a good ingredient in marriage or love, but it's probably not key for a successful conversation. What was the key factor for us? The interest and willingness to listen, even to someone who might just have ideas and experiences very different than his own.

The key wasn't the differences. Indeed, even after all of these years, we continue to disagree on many fundamental issues. They key was being open and respectful. And by respectful, we don't mean in the way you are supposed to respect your teacher or your parents. We mean respectful in that you can have a heated discussion with each other on the opposite sides of a topic that goes to the core of your belief system and still walk away at the end as friends. Raised voices—that's just because we each believe passionately we are correct. An attack—fine also, but on the idea, not the person. So not, "You're an asshole," but "The idea you're espousing is just completely wrong." These aren't meant as rules of engagement. Conversation doesn't work that way. You need to bring these qualities to the table. Your authors may have come from quite different worlds and might not have agreed on much and weren't bashful about telling the other he was "wrong" and why he was wrong. Yet it was always done without forgetting to listen to, and without forgetting to respect, the other person.

The result was not just a great conversation. As hard-headed as we each were and are, the listening and arguing also led our own opinions—which we had at one time, way back when, been so certain about—to evolve and to grow. We talk and we learn and never fear putting our ideas and beliefs to the test.

Life. We've already said that this is ultimately the topic that has driven our conversation and that drives any real conversation. What's it all about? Why do we live? What happens, if anything, after we die? Where is our world headed? And what is our own personal role in it all—hapless observers or potentially real factors for change? Do we even have a choice?

We each have children. One of them recently latched on to the idea that there is nothing about which he can be certain, absolutely nothing. The world is round—"That's what they say now, but maybe one day they will discover it is in fact flat." 2 + 2 = 4. "Just a concept that has been imposed on us." And, of course, don't even try to touch on subjects like God. The boy is a skeptic—in the radical form. He'll outgrow it? We certainly hope not. He actually came back a few days after first announcing that there was nothing about which one could be certain with proof of his position: On a flat surface, a triangle has a maximum of 180 degrees in three angles. But on a sphere, there can be a triangle with three 90-degree angles. This, despite what they teach in school: that a figure with three 90-degree angles must be a square (and that it must have a fourth 90-degree angle). There is actually a cool YouTube post that explains it all. And maybe even better than that, his math teacher was the one who encouraged him to further develop the idea that there is nothing about which we can be certain, even math equations. (And this, when his father and his father's friend in their own conversations were actually close to coming to an agreement that the only Truths—yes, with a capital T—are those arrived at by science and mathematics. We were proved wrong once again.)

Skepticism, like any belief system, isn't meant to be outgrown like a pair of jeans—or, using another clothes-related metaphor, they shouldn't be outgrown like the latest fashion. They should be thought about, thoroughly. Read books on the topic. Discuss with your teachers and family and friends. Start conversations to explore what others think and see whether your ideas hold water to the tough criticism of others. Consider and reconsider. Skepticism will happen.

We believe that considering these sorts of Big Questions matters. They have been an important part of our thirty-year conversation—an enjoyable, as well as enlightening, part. We actually believe that we are not at all exceptional, that most people, given the opportunity (or if they would make the opportunity), are interested in these questions. Questions and feelings and beliefs about Life are not just for philosophers. The only advantage philosophers have, if they are actually able to make a living at it, is the privilege of focusing much of their time on these questions. The vast majority of us aren't so lucky. The questions are forced on us—someone dies who is close to us, we read in the newspaper about some horrific crime, or we witness something of immense natural beauty. We then begin asking ourselves and those around us about Life and what it means. We are reminiscing with old friends, and the memories and sentiments lead us to ask questions about our own and our friends' lives, where we have been, and where we are going and why. It is beautiful. Of course, it can at the same time be tragic and sad. But as we try to delve into the essence of ourselves and others and the world around us, we are at our best – curious, thinking, exploring. "The most beautiful and deepest experience a man can have is the sense of the mysterious. It is the underlying principle of religion as well as all serious endeavor in art and sciences. He who never had this experience seems to me, if not dead, then at least blind."[23]

So, after thirty years of conversation, have we found the answers to all of those Big Questions we've been discussing? You'll need to wait for our next book to find out. For now, we are just enjoying the process. And we suggest that others also partake more in real conversation. As to whether we've figured it all out, if you really insist on an answer, we'll just say that we will never admit it because it's just way too much fun arguing. More seriously, though, we'll make clear that what we are advocating is not the way to "figure everything out," as if that were even possible. Rather, we are talking about a way to look at others, a way to see yourself in this complicated world of ours, and a way to live your life or at least enrich the way

---

[23] Albert Einstein, *My Credo*, 1932

you lead your life. Real conversation is part of really living. It is as essential as the air we breathe. Just look at the world today, literally dying, as real conversation at best struggles to survive. People and societies not engaged in real conversation are rapidly killing off themselves and those around them. We no longer connect and converse; we no longer think rationally and logically but instead are imprisoned by outdated and dangerous beliefs and traditions; we are left to die and, in destroying ourselves, also destroy the world around us.

Your authors' personal biographies may tell at least part of the story. Conversation has been an integral part of our work. We've spent (and gotten paid for spending) the bulk of our time away from stuffy corporate offices. We had to meet people, keep in touch with many of them, and develop close relationships with some, as part of our jobs. That certainly must have contributed to our view of conversation. For as long as we remember, connecting and speaking with people has been a way of life, fueled initially by the demands of the job but quickly transforming into a comfortable and satisfying way to engage with others. Speaking openly, asking questions, not accepting answers at face value, asking more questions, being careful to fully listen to what was being said—all this was demanded of us but also actually just felt like the right thing to do. Why not listen to all sides of the issue, and then check out the facts and arguments being presented, before drawing conclusions? Take a leader—political, spiritual, or business—at his or her word? We would never dream of it. Be concerned about offending someone's sensibilities, sure, but only if the person wasn't trying to make others proscribe to what he or she saw as the proper ways to act or think. If people were trying to impose their will on others, then they were fair game to be questioned and criticized. Real conversation is tough. Strong egos must be tamed. It's not easy to put one's beliefs to the test in conversation.

But before getting to the conversation, there is the meeting and the connection. Your authors met in a newsroom thousands of miles from where they were born and grew up. They've spent most of their adult lives exploring new places and meeting new people. It has been fun. But it did begin as work, which demanded international travel and engaging with people in all parts of the world. The "other" for us has always been something of great interest. We've wanted to engage with others to learn from what they thought, what they believed, and what they could show us of their communities. We knew that accepting, engaging, and opening up to others and getting them to open up to us were the right things to do, but these acts were also demanded of us.

The world of the early decades of the twenty-first century is one of divisions and rivalries. People are rarely looking for bridges and seem to almost always be striving for further separation. To engage with the Other is seen as dangerous. To build walls and fences to "protect against" the Other seems to make much more sense. Except, of course, if you've come to understand that Others are normally not threats, and even when they are, they are far less dangerous than presented by the rabble-rousers fueling dissent and distrust.

Maybe this is something else about ourselves we should let you in on. We have spent years living and working on the lovely east Mediterranean island of Cyprus. In recent years, our work has also brought us more and more often to the Cypriots' compatriots in Greece. Hellenic societies have given the world beautiful places and beautiful people and beautiful ideas and culture (and did we say food?). We certainly have been touched by this society. Our love for good food and drink and conversation certainly at least in part results from our love for Cyprus and Greece. We had an interest in good literature and philosophy previously, but add to that interest the smell of a lemon tree in a small village house courtyard in the Troodos Mountains or the cool breeze at a seaside restaurant in Athens, and the narratives of Homer and Plato quickly take on new meaning. Our many Greek and Greek Cypriot friends—in particular, the older ones—have an uncanny hold on their great history and culture. For us, the Greek thinkers are people we learned about in school and university. For our Greek and Greek Cypriot friends, these philosophers seem to be part of their upbringing and tradition.

The concept of Europe without Greece that abounded at the height of the economic crisis of 2009 might have been a topic of conversation in New York or London, discussed as if it were just another issue unfolding in far-off lands. But where we were at the time, those conversations were filled with anger and disgust at a Europe that was so quick to consider giving up the very birthplace of European culture. You would not expect anything less. So when we had coffee in Athens with one of our circles of friends and acquaintances—former and current Greek military officers—they did not hide their anger at having their pensions and salaries drastically cut and ongoing threats to throw them out of the EU.

We mention this not to express our view or analysis on the subject but to point out that one thing has certainly driven your authors' thirty-year conversation: our worldviews have grown over the years as we actually saw more and more of the world. Our professional lives have taken us to places around the world that many would call exotic. Most important, our professions gave us the opportunity to interact with people from a wide range of cultures and backgrounds, and we were greatly enriched in the process. Yes, there are experiences and sites that will remain with us forever. But most significantly, there were conversations. We listened to, and interacted with, a wide range of people in a wide range of places, and we discussed endless topics, some mundane and others uplifting. We learned in the process. We also grew as individuals—and so did those with whom we interacted. This is the beauty of real conversation: It breaks the laws of physics. The energy in the interaction of real conversation is not preserved; rather, it grows. There are no losers. All are winners. This is not to say that all is "perfect" and that the conversations are always congenial and the topics, sugar-coated. Conversation can be painful. It can open your eyes to suffering and injustice and all things evil. Experiencing horror, even "just" through conversation, is part of what it means to be human. Real conversation is unfiltered. Maybe that's why it must happen in person. On Facebook or Instagram or WhatsApp, you see only what you choose in others, and you present yourself only as you want to be seen. In a real conversation, you sit down with someone and open up to that person and he or she to you. On one level, you don't really care what the individual thinks, in the sense that you are not trying to convince him or her of something or get the person to give you something. You simply open up and say exactly what you think and feel, then you stop and listen—listen sincerely to what the person has to say. No one is judging. Everyone is caring, deeply caring, even while perhaps disagreeing. That is all part of what conversation offers. That's what we've been lucky to have for so many years now—and we are sure that others have also experienced this, but not enough others. There are too many distractions, too many good excuses for avoiding real engagement. Perhaps even worse, in a world defined largely by power and money and other forms of materialistic wealth, it is hard to make time for something like conversation that, on the face of it, seems—well, let's say it bluntly—like a waste of time.

Just try telling your boss, "I'm headed off to lunch. Might not be back for two to three hours." Or say to your boyfriend or girlfriend, "I won't be back until late. Going to hang out with some friends for a bit."

"What exactly do you plan to do?" you might be asked. And what can you really answer, if not, "Nothing. Just talk"?

What a waste of time! We certainly have "wasted" a lot of time talking in those passing years. And yes, we admit, sometimes the topics were particularly "useless," like whether there is free will or if man is intrinsically evil or if the United States was justified in invading Iraq. What do our opinions matter, anyway? Who are we kidding, other than ourselves, by delving into such topics? We do have one strong comeback, however. Indeed, one that allows us to smugly sit back and order another round: How's that been working out, allowing the experts (read politicians, preachers, philosophers, etc.) to run things the way they think is best? Not too well, eh? So we'll keep talking, thank you. Our conversation has been going for three decades, but we feel like we've barely gotten started.

10 *From Socrates to Grandpa Jack*

> *It was impossible to get a conversation*
> *going, everybody was talking too much.*
> —Yogi Berra

SOME BIG NAMES have had their say about the importance of conversations. And these folks really upped the ante when it comes to assessing the importance of conversation, attributing to conversation the power to change the minds of gods and inspire the battle cries of revolutionaries. With so much at stake, the practitioners and the advocates of the powers of conversation through the ages—from Abraham and Job arguing with God to Socrates and Plato jousting with their students, to Freire's revolutionary dialogue and dialogism—all agreed that conversation could be transforming for both a person and a society.

BILL: THE TOASTMASTER'S TALE

For Grandpa Jack, conversation was an art. Or maybe an ability—one that needed to be honed and developed, something that should be learned as you learn other life skills.

Grandpa Jack was also a big advocate of Toastmasters. He had learned public speaking in one of their classes, and he was actually great at it. He realized that it was important to know how to stand up and speak in front of a crowd if he wanted to advance professionally. He knew he wasn't a natural, so he learned the key elements of public speaking and practiced them over and over, until he mastered them.

Now, Grandpa Jack didn't learn the "art of conversation" exactly in that manner. We don't want to digress into his personal history, which included hours in Jewish religious school studying Talmud and Torah and learning to argue the different nuances of Jewish religious law. But the result was the same: in these classes, conversation wasn't about connecting with someone else, it was about convincing them, showing them you were smarter, outwitting your rival in dialogue.

For those of us in his family who could put up with Grandpa Jack (and it is a poorly kept Hutman/Seidenberg family secret that many could not), we actually have much for which to thank him. Certainly, at least on one level, Grandpa taught us well: how to think on our feet, how to take on any side of an argument and make it our own to advocate for. If nothing else, this ability allowed us to see the other side of an issue. Remember, in one of Grandpa Jack's conversations you were always trying to outdo whoever else was sitting around the dinner table, arguing. You had to beat the person, and the only way to do that, of course, was to anticipate and then undermine any argument he or she presented.

For Grandpa Jack, conversation seemed to be a purely intellectual exercise. He was an expert at provoking you into a conversation. You never knew what he actually believed. It was if he would eye his potential partner in dialogue and slowly ascertain what provocative statement he could make that would draw the person into conversation.

His favorite topics were those connected to Judaism. His parents had immigrated to the United States from Eastern Europe. They were religious Jews. Yet like many of his contemporaries born of religious Jewish parents, Jack was secular. He almost never went to synagogue. Even on the major Jewish holidays, he'd stay home. God was of little interest to him. Indeed, everyone just assumed he was an atheist. Yet that never stopped him from taking the most orthodox positions in his arguments, knowing that (just like him) the younger people around the table were easy prey to such comments as "You know, Jews really are a chosen people," or in one instance that got him a great reaction, "Jews throughout history were much cleaner than other people. That's what saved us from the plagues."

And then the conversation would begin, always heated and emotional. It frequently ended with someone stomping out of the room, furious. Yet it was often thought-provoking as well. Grandpa made us realize that politics and religion could actually be interesting and engaging topics to talk about. And while many times he simply made us mad at him (and at each other), I can't begin to say how much we learned in those conversations, as we argued about whatever topic had caught his and our imagination. The topics were normally taken from the daily news—certainly not too bad of a thing.

There was actually another fun element in the "art of conversation" in Grandpa Jack's heyday of the 1970s and the 1980s. There was no Internet yet. No Google. No instant fact checking. Yes, Grandpa had an *Encyclopedia Britannica* at home, a dictionary, and a bunch of other books. But for the most part we had to trust one another that we weren't simply making things up. So, was it all just fake news? No. Lots of wrong "facts" were certainly thrown around in these conversations that almost always turned into arguments. But it is probably fair to say that in most cases, these came from honest mistakes. Anyone who could put up with Grandpa Jack, however, did quickly learn that a key element of the "art of conversation" was presenting your view in a convincing manner. This meant not only stating it clearly, but also speaking with confidence. And confidence didn't simply mean the way you spoke and your mannerisms, but you had to manifest the telltale expressions of someone who appeared to know what he or she was talking about. We had to pepper our arguments with the right examples and details to at least give the impression that we were knowledgeable about the topic.

What we can all learn from this type of conversation is that despite its being fun and engaging, what it lacks is truly tragic when we look at it on a personal level. For what do we learn about others and even about ourselves when we are simply trying to outwit one another? Perhaps there are opportunities in such conversations to open up, but they are rare and, at their essence, contrary to the very nature of this type of conversation. Whenever we do open up or listen to others speaking about something personal as they present their argument, the purpose of the exercise is to convince them of one thing or another. This is not a sincere opening up or sincere listening. It is just a tactic and a counter-tactic.

* * * * * *

Perhaps the most famous practitioner of conversation was Socrates, as recorded by his student Plato. Socrates's dialogues were not conversations among equals. It was clear from the outset and throughout the dialogues who was the boss. Wisdom was the domain of Socrates. His companions in conversation might at times have had something interesting to say, but ultimately it was Socrates who had the last word. Socrates utilized conversation to analyze and discuss a particular topic, but it is clear that he had control. He knew where the conversation would lead. He was the wise teacher; they were the pupils there to learn from the Master. "My dear fellow, what is there left for me or for anyone to say, after such a fine and varied speech?"[24] Socrates plays the humble listener. "Wasn't I right when I predicted Agathon would make a brilliant speech, and there would be nothing left for me to say?"

But who was he kidding? We have already gotten to know Socrates well enough to understand that this was all part of the game. "Your prediction was only half true," Eryximachus chimes in right on cue, just as Socrates appears to be saying the last word has gone to someone other than him. "Agathon did make a good speech. But I don't think you will find nothing to say." And Socrates does find something to say. We then watch

---

[24] Plato, *Symposium and the Death of Socrates* (Wordsworth Classics of World Literature, 1997), p. 30.

as, in perfect form and using the "Socratic method," he takes apart Agathon's earlier statements (but didn't Socrates just say Agathon should have the last word on the topic?), until he corners Agathon and forces him to admit defeat.

Agathon: I can't argue with you, Socrates. Let's take it that it is as you say.

Socrates: What you mean, Agathon, my dear friend, is that you can't argue with the truth. Any fool can argue with Socrates.

A bit arrogant, perhaps, but Socrates is making an important point: Have the courage to express your opinions, to argue them in the company of your friends, classmates, or colleagues. Put your ideas to the test of logic and reason—not your own, but with others in conversation and discussion. See whether your ideas withstand the test. And if they don't, be courageous enough to admit you were mistaken. Don't take it personally. Even if there was a mistake made in your analysis, it is not a reflection on you. It is only a reflection on the idea presented. "You can't argue with the truth."

The catch in Plato's dialogues is that in all of the conversations, just one guy seems to know what the truth is. Others in the conversation are allowed to voice their opinions and even say interesting things, but the truth is held by just one man. The conversation is not between equals.

Now Socrates was admittedly a smart guy—one might even go so far as to say the wisest of his time. So listening to what he has to say makes sense. It is certainly nice that he also does some listening and allows others to express their opinions. He challenges us to use our own minds. "The unexamined life is not worth living," he tells us. His plea for the freedom to think and use reason and not just accept the dictates of our peers or those in power was revolutionary. It is a plea that has echoed through the ages all the way to our times, in which, sadly, the voices of ignorance and bias continue to prevail in so many realms.

Socrates chose death over giving up conversation. That is certainly something to ponder, particularly at a time like now, when reason and open dialogue seem so threatened.

Socrates drank the poison without hesitation. His friends cried. He did not. He didn't feel he had anything to cry for, as he had lived a life and now had arrived at a death that were both of his choosing.

> This made us ashamed, and we stopped crying. As for Socrates, he walked around, and when he said his legs were getting heavy, he lay down on his back, as the man had told him to. The chill had just about reached his abdomen when he uncovered his face, which he had covered up, and said—and these were the last words he uttered—"Crito, we owe a cock to Asceplius. Pay the debt. Don't forget."[25]

Had Socrates cheated us in the end, his last breath spent expressing concern about making a sacrifice to the god of medicine, who was owed it in thanks for answering a previous petition, instead of sharing with us one last little bit of his

---

[25] Ibid., p. 210.

wisdom? Of course not. His final words were a reminder: Yes, reason and ideas are worth living and dying for, but just as important is being a good person, paying your debt, giving thanks.

To have a conversation, you must have a voice. For Socrates, the wise man of his time, that was easy. He was opinionated. He seemed to know that he was the smartest one around, so he spoke with confidence. Indeed, there are times when you think that he won't stop talking. But to his credit, he also allows his pupils to have a voice. That is no small matter. There always have been the speakers and those spoken to. There is the king or the president who, due to authority vested on him by the gods or by the people, is the one who sets the tone of conversation and indeed controls it to the degree that he is able. To raise your voice, to express a different opinion, is to be a revolutionary. It is to be powerful and confident. It is to be fearless. How much easier it is to remain silent, leave it to others to speak out when they see wrong. To speak out can be dangerous. It can get you in trouble. In silence, there is safety and comfort.

So you have a choice: Keep quiet or join the conversation.

Socrates beckoned his pupils to join the conversation. It took some persuading at times. Perhaps it always does, in the face of authority. It would have been so much easier for the pupils at the lyceum to have remained quiet—to simply listen and obey. But Socrates knew better. He understood that true learning—the kind of learning from which critical and creative thinking is developed—comes through conversation.

Yet what about rote learning, the pupils sitting silently, writing down the teacher's every word and then putting it to memory? The Ancient Greeks, nearly 3,000 years ago, had already realized that this was no way to learn. How sad that in our own age, there still remain many schools and education systems that rely on this method. Instead of teaching children to think, they try to stuff as many facts as possible into their heads. We will speak more later about the great modern educator and revolutionary Paulo Freire, who fought hard against his own country's oppressive education system and was exiled for it. Freire was a great advocate of conversation, seeing it as an essential tool in education, as did the Greeks. How pitiful that this is still a point of contention nearly three millennia after Socrates.

Much has been written about the human tendency toward authoritarianism. Adolf Hitler was an elected leader. Russian communists turned an ideology whose very essence calls for the freedom of the masses into a ruthless totalitarian regime. And now, in the early twenty-first century, we see governments from the Americas to Europe, to the Middle East and Asia, including such one-time stalwart supporters of political freedom as the United States, openly embracing ideologies and policies that would make a fascist proud.

> Can freedom become a burden, too heavy for man to bear, something he tries to escape from? Is there not also, perhaps, besides an innate desire for freedom, an instinctive wish for submission? If there is not, how can we account for the attraction which submission to a leader has for so many to-day? Is submission always to an overt authority or is there also submission to internalized authorities, such as duty

or conscience, to inner compulsions or to anonymous authorities like public opinion? Is there a hidden satisfaction in submitting, and what is its essence?[26]

Maybe that's just the way we humans are built. We don't like freedom. We prefer the security of obedience. We prefer the security of silence. And most certainly, it would seem, we believe that survival means looking out for own interests, no matter what expense to the "other."

It should be no wonder that conversation—real, open conversation that is at the root of not only personal freedom but also political freedom—has had such a rough time of it. Do we really want our children to think freely? Freire answers a resounding, "Yes." Many others give it lip service. Yet it would appear that most of us prefer to be told what to do. Silence and obedience are just so much easier options.

Let's return to the ancients. We (the authors) often like to return to the ancient world when considering issues facing our world today. We find credence in the famous pronouncement in Ecclesiastes "There is nothing new under the sun." Just as in Greece in the millennium before Christ they were making breakthroughs in science and reason that continue to provide the basis for our way of thinking today, so, too, did ancient civilizations elsewhere of the same era appear to have had similar insights. The wisdom of Ecclesiastes eventually made it into the Hebrew and Christian scriptures, accepted by Jews and Christians and, to a great extent, also Muslims, as providing

---

[26] Erich Fromm, *The Fear of Freedom* (London: Routledge Classics, 1942), p. 4.

part of the underlying value structure on which society should be built. "Love your neighbor as yourself"; "Thou shall not murder"; "Honor your father and mother." The insight offered in these ancient texts is powerful. The cry that comes out in many of these books and stories for a more just and peaceful world is loud and clear. Or so it might seem. The truth—or, at least, the truth as played out in human history—offers a quite different view of what these texts, and especially these texts as the basis of religious and political hierarchies, offered the world. Indeed, great effort is required when looking back through history to find the messages of goodwill and peace. More often, we find oppression and even evil, from Crusades and holy wars to inquisitions and pogroms. The victims were many—Jews and Muslims and even other Christians. Religion may have within its text enlightening ideas, but in society, it has given us much darkness.

The conversations are uplifting in many key parts of the Hebrew scriptures and later were also adopted into Christianity and Islam and became, as such, pillars of Western thought. Adam and Eve ignore God's orders, then eat the forbidden fruit that empowers them to differentiate between good and evil. The message is clear. If they had obeyed God's orders, yes, they could have continued life in the Garden of Eden. But they would have also left us with a world bereft of moral and ethical content: people without an understanding of right and wrong. Adam and Eve's choice was, of course, inevitable, their creation myth reflecting the outcome that its authors and transmitters saw in the world around them—a world where people had a choice between good and evil. So, why didn't God just create us from the beginning that way and simply do away with the need for the Garden of Eden story? Maybe He was merely in need of a good conversation. The scriptures are filled with them: The Hebrews and their leaders in an ongoing back and forth with God. Abraham convinces God, at least for a while, to hold off destroying Sodom. Moses at first refuses his Calling. And even the righteous Job questions his Maker. To say nothing about the Hebrews themselves. No sooner had God freed them from Egyptian bondage than they wanted to head back. The scene is powerful one. Pharaoh has had second thoughts and with his army is in hot pursuit of the Hebrews. He has just about caught up with them. The Hebrews barely make it across the Red Sea, waters divided by their all-powerful God. They watch as Pharaoh and his army are crushed under the waves when the Red Sea waters return. And then, just several verses later, they are whining again, begging to be returned to Egypt as they look out on the vast desert and fear they will lack food and water and therefore die. The reader or the person hearing this tale wouldn't be out of line in asking, "Were the Hebrews out of their minds? They just saw the dividing of the Red Sea and the crushing of Pharaoh and his army, and they still doubted God's ability to feed and protect them? Crazy." Or maybe not so crazy? The tales we have in the Bible are rarely lessons in obedience and blind faith. Rather, they are tales of searching— searching for a way to survive and, once people survive, how best to live as individuals and as societies.

> Revelation does not happen when God is alone. It was both an event in the life of God and an event in the life of man. without the power to respond, without the fact that there was a people willing to accept, to hear, the divine command, Sinai

would have been impossible. For Sinai consisted of both a divine proclamation and a human perception. It was a moment in which God was not alone.[27]

Even with God, there is conversation. "The Bible contains not only records of what transpired in moments of prophetic inspiration; it is also records acts and words of man. Thus the Bible is more than the word of God: It is the word of God and man."[28]

The scriptures can be read as rulebooks. They can be read as setting down strict laws for individual behavior and the structure of society. They can be used to justify oppression of the "rule-breakers" and can force obedience on those who claim the authority of having the one true understanding of God's will. History is filled with political and religious leaders who made this claim and used it to the evil outcomes one would expect that such ideology would bring. But this is a wrong reading.

The ancient Hebrews could witness God's miracles and still question Him, but we can't? The scriptures are full of tales of people pushing back against God's will. The message is clear. We aren't being told to shut up and do what we are told. We are being told to explore and question. The message is revolutionary—if we can question the Almighty, then what can we not question? The answer would seem to be that there should be no limits to our inquiry. The conversation should have no limits.

---

[27] Ibid., p. 260.
[28] Ibid., p. 260.

Religion, tragically, has come to stand on the side of fascism and oppression. It has worked to stamp out real conversation. When a religion denies conversation in favor of dogma in its own texts, it can only be expected to demand the same from society. The religious establishment should be held responsible for this tragic state. It has imprisoned the beautiful, inspiring texts and traditions. It is our job to try to set them free. On the other side, on the side of freedom, it has been long replaced by reason. In reason, philosophy and science and free thinking—and, yes, real conversation—can all, to an extent at least, find a safe haven.

> Reason is one with the boundless will to communication. Reason refused to break off communication. If the break in the sphere of existence is brought about by force, it can never recognize this as fundamentally necessary. With imperturbable confidence in the boundless possibilities of the whole of Being, Reason demands that the risk of communication should be taken again and again. To deny communication is tantamount to denying Reason itself.[29]

Yes, conversation involves risk. Your underlying beliefs may be shaken. Your eyes may be opened to worlds you would perhaps prefer never to have known or experienced. With this

---

[29] Karl Jaspers, *Reason and Anti-Reason in Our Time: The Struggle for Man's Mind* (New Haven: Yale University Press, 1952), pp. 42–43.

comes insecurity and fear. Fear of the unknown. Fear of the unexplained or what would appear to be the unexplainable. If we allow it, the trail of conversation may lead to an abyss: the only way forward is a fall, a bad fall. But it doesn't have to be this way, nor in any way should it "naturally" lead in that direction. The challenge that real conversation brings can and should be an uplifting one. Rather than a fall into the abyss, it can lead us to know heights.

Freedom is uplifting. It looks scary at first glance—very scary. When you are willing to question everything; when you refuse to accept certain religious, cultural, political, and scientific ideas and even "facts" that must be seen as "Truths" that must be accepted and cannot be accepted, you might seem to be heading toward an unstable place. You become an easy target. You will be accused of betrayal, betraying your country, religion, family, and the list goes on. You are a traitor. You are alone. Even the company of others like yourself is no refuge. They, too, are traitors. They can't be trusted. There is nothing that binds you together. Distrust can only break people apart. It can't bring them together.

It is indeed a scary place to be. Armed with curiosity (skepticism?) and eager to question, you would appear to have nothing on which to get your bearings. Even language fails you. Armed knowingly or unknowingly (you don't have to have read them to have grasped the concepts and implications) with the weapons of the structuralists and the post-structuralists that lead the battle not just against Knowledge but also against language, all that appears left is void: empty, dark.

Here is where we are saved by conversation. In its very essence, there is no form to conversation. Yes, there are words and tones of speech, but they are relatively easily plied.

They provide harder targets for deconstruction. Indeed, at its very essence, it might be said that real conversation is deconstructive. No one has the last word. Ideas and words and we as individuals are given the opportunity in conversation to grow and change. We aren't talking with any clear aim in mind. We let our thoughts roam. Yes, we push back. We are critical of our own ideas and those being discussed. We let our minds think and ponder. We explore. We are free. What joy! And don't take our word for it. "To my taste the most fruit and most natural exercise of our minds is conversation," explains the great sixteenth-century philosopher and essayist Michel de Montaigne.

> I find the practice of it the most delightful activity of our lives. If I am sparring with a strong and solid opponent he will attack me on the flanks, stick his lance in me right and left; his ideas send mine soaring. Rivalry, competitiveness and glory will drive me and raise me above my own level. In conversation the most painful quality is perfect harmony.[30]

You need a partner, and the partner must be a "partner in crime" if it is going to be a real conversation. Nothing is too sacred to be discussed. No opinion too "wrong" to mention. No idea too "stupid." Speak freely. Listen. Discuss. Slow down. Don't be afraid to think . . . and not to act or even explain.

---

[30] Michel de Montaigne, *Essays: On Friendship,* (London: Penguin Books, 2004), p. 32.

Be courageous enough to put your ideas to the test. Indeed, it shouldn't even cross your mind not to mention something, if the conversation is a real one. And if it is a real conversation, you must be emotionally engaged. You must care about what's being talked about. Sometimes you must care so much, you feel like punching the other person in the face. Or you almost get up and walk away. (Our apologies to Montaigne because, in our view, there are things more painful than harmony that can result from conversation.) But don't do either. Keep seated. Try to listen. No one said you must agree.

An example: The late Nazi-hunter Simon Wiesenthal's encounter with an SS officer. The encounter is detailed in Wiesenthal's *The Sunflower: On the Possibilities and Limits of Forgiveness*. The book starts with his story of his chance meeting with a hospitalized SS officer while a prisoner at a death camp and the officer asking Wiesenthal for forgiveness. The book then includes short essays from leading theologians and thinkers from a wide range of backgrounds. The contributing essayists are asked whether Wiesenthal should have forgiven the officer and are requested to comment on the topic of forgiveness in light of the atrocities of the Holocaust. The essays are interesting and insightful, but overlooked is the conversation itself.

Wiesenthal encountered the hospitalized SS soldier while on a concentration camp work detail. He did not have to speak to the SS officer. While we don't really know for sure, it might even be surmised that Wiesenthal could have killed the officer (who was badly injured, and it might have been enough to smother him in his hospital bed). Instead, they spoke. Wiesenthal, fully aware of the terrible atrocities done by the Nazis and the SS in particular, willingly listened as the young man tried to explain how he got caught up in the war and joined the elite Nazi brigade. He looked to Wiesenthal, as a Jew, for forgiveness for the evil he now, on his deathbed, recognized that he had done. Yet the glaring question seems to be why should Wiesenthal have even spoken with the young man, an SS officer who admitted to killing innocent Jews?

Wiesenthal has given us his answer in the very writing of the book. There is no one with whom we shouldn't enter into conversation. We don't need to agree with what they say. We don't have to forgive, if asked, although we may. But we can listen. We can also learn and grow, even from a conversation with someone who has done great evil.

11

An Enemy We'd Better Befriend

A new survey says 64 percent of Americans
own a smartphone. Interesting!
In a related survey, 100 percent of
smartphones say they own an American.
— Jimmy Fallon

THE SCENE IS repeated everywhere. From train stations and airports to dinner tables and doctors' offices and parks, the scene is the same: all heads are down. No one is making eye contact or even just looking around. What has their attention? The phones they are holding a few inches from their faces. The phenomenon became bad enough for the BBC to launch a "Crossing Divides on the Move" initiative in the summer of 2019 aimed at "encouraging adults to chat" with fellow commuters. The UK's national media company convinced some of the country's railroad operators to designate certain coaches as "chat coaches," and to encourage people to "share a smile" and "people from different backgrounds to mix."

The BBC also conducted its own research in both the United States and the United Kingdom that showed "those randomly assigned to talk (to strangers) had the most pleasant commute," when compared to those who sat in solitude.[31] And if that weren't enough to demonstrate what should be common sense—that connecting with people in general makes one feel good—there are academic studies that also supported the conclusion, such as this one from the University of Chicago, quoted in the same BBC article:

> "Connecting with others increases happiness, but strangers in close proximity routinely ignore each other. Why? Two reasons seem likely: either solitude is a more positive experience than interacting with strangers, or people misunderstand the consequences of distant social connections.
>
> To examine the experience of connecting to strangers, we instructed commuters on trains and buses to connect with a stranger near them, to remain disconnected, or to commute as normal (Experiments 1a and 2a). In both contexts, participants reported a more positive (and no less productive) experience when they connected than when they did not. Separate participants in each context, however, expected precisely the opposite outcome, predicting a more positive experience in

---

[31] See www.bbc.co.uk/news/world-48459940

solitude (Experiments 1b and 2b). This mistaken preference for solitude stems partly from underestimating others' interest in connecting (Experiments 3a and 3b), which in turn keeps people from learning the actual consequences of social interaction (Experiments 4a and 4b). The pleasure of connection seems contagious: In a laboratory waiting room, participants who were talked to had equally positive experiences as those instructed to talk (Experiment 5). Human beings are social animals. Those who misunderstand the consequences of social interactions may not, in at least some contexts, be social enough for their own well-being.[32]"

Common sense tells us it's good to connect. There is no need for conducting academic studies to know that. We know this from our lives. We don't need an academic study to tell us whether it's better to be hiding our faces in our smartphones, as opposed to speaking to the person sitting next to us.

That said, we'd like to avoid simply jumping on the bandwagon of the so-called experts who have accused the smartphone of just about every current human ill. Fake news, breakdown of the family, childhood depression. What hasn't the smartphone been accused of?

---

[32] Nicholas Epley and Juliana Schroeder, University of Chicago, "Mistakenly Seeking Solitude," *Journal of Experimental Psychology* 143, no. 5 (2014).

So why don't we just add one more thing? Smartphone use is undercutting the close person-to-person contact that real conversation brings. When you're focused on your phone for most of the day, it goes without saying that you can't even get a conversation started. Why strike up a conversation with the other person waiting at the bus stop when you both are unaware of anyone around you, you're so preoccupied with checking WhatsApp messages? Sitting at a bar, you used to have no choice but to at least exchange a few words with the guy or the gal beside you.

Today, just keep your eyes focused on the screen. And up come the walls separating us from those around us. It's hard not to bash smartphone use. It's an easy target, but perhaps too easy. And if not too easy, also somewhat useless. What do you plan to do, prevent people from using their smartphones? Limit the number of hours a day they can use one? Yeah, like that would ever work, if we'd even want to give it a try. Many a well-intentioned parent forbade or greatly limited their toddlers' television viewing, only to throw up their arms when it became clear that nothing was going to stop their kids from watching TV.

And why should they stop using their smartphones anyway? Being online is being connected—with your friends from class, your old friends from the old school you went to before moving, or to your grandparents and uncles and aunts whom you see much less often since your parents moved you all overseas. There is literally no way you could stay in touch with so many friends and family if staying in touch meant meeting with them.

And what about opportunities to make new friends? Can you beat social media for that? Talk about expanding your social horizons. Yes, a lot of those connections are pure decadence—and at times of the worst kind. Like most anything that has good uses, social media also has other uses that are not as positive. That doesn't mean we give up on something just because it has some negative aspects. We just need to teach ourselves and then our children the right uses and how to stick to them.

Think of the numerous social causes driven by technologies that allow us to converse easily and quickly with people not just from our immediate community but throughout whatever country we may live in, to people around the world.

Similarly, think of the political causes sparked by social media and the ability—indeed, the power—it gives to the otherwise disenfranchised.

Talk about the power of technology-empowered conversations. It is undeniable. Indeed, its power is frightening. These technology-empowered conversations build not only bonds, but also movements; they move people to action, to change. Herein lies the strength and potential of the technology-empowered conversation. Herein, too, is where it in essence parts from the type of conversation we are advocating.

Remember that at the very core of our definition lies impracticality. You don't enter into conversation in order to "do something" or "get something." Such conversation is in the realm of I-It. In such conversations, we are each a means to an end. That end may be good. It may help improve our neighborhood or society. It is clearly by definition not in and of itself "bad." Yet it falls short of real conversation.

Real conversation is rooted in connection, not action. It may lead to action, but it at least begins with opening up to the other; listening but not judging; listening with no goal in mind other than making yourself sensitive to the person you are speaking with, as she must also listen to you. Growing? Yes. But growing in the purest fashion: bringing about no material change. The growth is in the self only, in the self of each of the parties involved in the conversation. You are growing—becoming a better person, a more complete person—as you can only become through relationships.

The experience is spiritual. Not religious, but spiritual. Not material—or, at least, not material in any manner that we understand today. In the future, will there be a pill we can take to replace the human need for real conversation? That is an interesting question, one that touches on the root of the current debate between those who advocate a purely material view of the world and those who cling to a more spiritual view (and here, "spiritual" includes "religious" but is not limited to it). For now at least, we know of no alternative to real conversation, no material alternative for its essential contribution to making someone a more complete person.

Which returns us to the topic of this chapter: technology. Conversation in its most basic form is process. So, too, in many ways are certain technologies and, in particular, those related to communication like the smartphone. Texts, WhatsApp, mobile voice conversations, Skype calls—these and countless others are processes through which we communicate today.

And at least today, not one of these technologies replaces face-to-face intimate conversation.

You must be together with someone; the setting must be intimate enough where you can speak openly; the atmosphere, one in which you can put aside, if even just for a few moments, the immediate material world and, through talk, dive deep into yourself and the self of your friend.

Let's put our theory to a test. Let's look at a conversation that not in theory but in practicality could be conducted either over social media or in person: There have been a few stories in the news recently on whether male-to-female transgender athletes should be able to compete competitively—for instance, in the Olympics. The topic is certainly interesting. There would appear to be lots of different opinions that could be voiced on the topic. And it certainly is a topic that touches on larger issues of the day, as they relate to gender identity. So it's not surprising that the social media "lights up" on the issue. Everyone wants to have a say and to voice his or her opinion. But is there real conversation? Is there even dialogue going on as Facebook posts mount?

Just look at what happened to tennis legend Martina Navratilova when she jumped into the fray. And there wasn't much of what we think anyone would define as conversation when she did. Navratilova took the public stand that it would be unfair to allow male-to-female transgender athletes to compete professionally against other women. "I am happy to address a transgender woman in whatever form she prefers, but I would not be happy to compete against her. It would not be fair," she wrote. And she was crucified for it. She was fired from an LBGT group for which she had done advocacy work. Her comments should have started an interesting conversation. People could have presented their opinions, their views for or against. This could have been peppered with personal stories that relate to the issue. Those with access or knowledge of scientific data could have added to the discussion. Different views could have been presented, critiqued, perhaps blown apart, or even developed. But this is not what happens when the forum for conversation is social media. In Facebook and

WhatsApp chat groups, the exchange quickly becomes personal and ugly. There is little discussion and much name-calling.

Even worse, there is shaming. What is too often attacked in social media is not the idea, but the person who holds it. People are made to feel stupid. They are ostracized.

In social media today, there is little room for real conversation. There are forums we join in order to hear from liked-minded people. There are others we join to bash those who think differently than us. Real conversation is hard to find. Is the technology to blame, or are we humans the problem? We don't know. (There's a topic for conversation.)

It will not be long before those who now have bad conversations with one another will be able to have bad conversations with their technology. We're almost there— "Siri, what are you wearing?" Google's Duplex is a sort of artificial-intelligence (AI) assistant that can make phone calls for you. Its finest achievement so far has been to book a haircut appointment without the receptionist knowing it wasn't human. (Big deal—few receptionists we speak to ever treat us as human.) There's still some ways to go before Duplex will join you at the barber shop and chime in with "How about that Liverpool goal last night?" or inquire whether "you'd like something for the weekend?" (Wink!)

In 2018, IBM rolled out Project Debater, its advance on Deep Blue, the chess player, and Watson, the *Jeopardy* quiz whiz. (Internet wags at once renamed it the Master Debater.) The machine was generally agreed to have performed well enough in two brief debates with humans, but its robotic female voice and rectangular black-box body language (none) aren't getting it invited to any dinner parties soon. "I love talking about nothing," said master-debater Oscar Wilde, "it is the only thing

I know anything about." So, a Wilde might be the best person to converse with a robot. Like Seinfeld, most AI conversation programs seem to be about nothing, mere exchanges of data between networks.

Google's director of engineering and AI expert Ray Kurzweil says technologies like IBM's Watson are only the beginning: "One does not need to be an AI expert to be moved by the performance of Watson on *Jeopardy*! Although I have a reasonable understanding of the methodology subsystems, that does not diminish my emotional reaction to watching it (him?) perform." Kurzweil goes on to rebuff the naysayers of conversational technologies: "The complaints reminded me of the story of the dog who plays chess. To an incredulous questioner, the dog's owner replies, 'Yeah, it's true, he does play chess, but his endgame is weak.'"

Kurzweil envisions a world of fast-advancing technologies and an eventual convergence of human and AI evolution. The future (or near future, even), according to Kurzweil, will include communication technologies that can't be told apart from actual human conversation and that suggest possibilities for "upgrading" human intelligence through technology. He's likely on the mark and perhaps sooner than the short time line he currently predicts.

Project Debater could not absorb more than four minutes of speech at a time. That may sound no worse than the average teenager, but there's a lot more to conversation than mechanically discussing whether NASA should go to Mars (one of the debater's topics). Human conversation is fragmented, unpredictable, with topics forking off in odd directions. There are flashes of irritation, outbreaks of laughter, ums, aahs, and repetitions. Since the arrival of a universal encyclopedia in our pockets, no one has become more irritating than the smart-ass who always checks your facts on Google—a real conversation stopper. Conversation is more akin to storytelling than fact spouting. People don't chat to swap facts and accurate minutiae. They do so to share feelings and experiences, and, at their best, they want to understand one another. Studies suggest that women talk to form bonds, building and maintaining their social network. Men talk about themselves or things they know a lot about, often to impress people around them.

Conversations are about whatever comes to mind, unrelated to how interesting it is. What usually comes to mind are the everyday things in our current environment, sometimes important (to us), but mostly trivial. It is on this organic human web that technology wreaks havoc, and it's not just the couple texting elsewhere or the moron looking up your current ailment on Wikipedia. Even if two people sit with their silenced phones lying on the table, the mere presence of the devices changes the quality of conversation. There are furtive, probably unconscious, glances at the phones, inhibiting the natural flow of chatter—because these two think they're about to be interrupted. The silent phone is like the hovering boss who might say, "Can I have a word?" or the partner about to say, "We have to talk." They all really mean "You're going to have to listen to this," and that bodes ill for any further pleasurable conversation.

The future is the future, but what we do know now is that the old-fashioned version of conversation works pretty well. Indeed, it works very well from any number of perspectives. Most important, we can grow through it, rather than feel abused and hurt by it, as is more than likely with a "conversation" on Facebook or a WhatsApp group.

No matter what your view of Navratilova's position on transgender athletes, we know you'd rather discuss it with her in person than exchange messages on a WhatsApp group. Short of that, wouldn't it be interesting and maybe even edifying to discuss the topic with friends or colleagues? That's if we still have such circles of friends and acquaintants with whom we have real conversations, if we haven't become like most people and if we have any opinions at all, the main place we voice them is via media.

We've forgotten how to talk. Or for the younger of us, we may have never learned because the main form of communication we've always known is via our phones.

So, must conversations be of the "old-fashioned" type? Today the answer is a resounding "Yes!"

Yet we are less confident that this is the final word. Technologies are advancing—and fast. And we humans are slow. It takes us time to fully adapt to a technology, even though we may be quick to acquire it. Owning is not mastering. And with technologies connected to communication, at issue is not our ability (i.e ., mastering how to use that new app on our phones), but fully integrating the technology into our worldview.

But humans are good at adapting, in particular when it is something like a new technology that overall makes our lives easier and is simple to use. So one day, perhaps even soon, we may be able to have a real conversation on whatever gadget, smartphone or otherwise, has made personal contact perhaps not obsolete, but at least less of a requirement.

In the meantime, we hope to see you more often in your neighborhood bar or cafe, with a favorite beverage and a good friend chatting away and the phone turned off (or at least put on silent mode).

* * * * * *

Before you get to talking, though, wait a bit. Listen. Listen to nothing at all.

Silence. There is something about the very word. It enchants, beckons, and beguiles. It is a word that should not exist because the moment it is uttered, it disappears. There it is; there it's gone. There is nothing that can express it because to express silence is to annihilate it.

If conversation is at the essence of being human, where does that leave silence? How can we consider the importance of conversation without also considering its antithesis? And perhaps that is the very point: that we need conversation, and we also need silence, like yin and yang. They together complete the circle, and they both have been largely lost in modern society. We must recapture them if we are to regain our souls. Ponder silence. Try to find it. Halt your inner voice. Close your eyes. Listen. You can't silence what is outside of you. The silence can only be from within, and even that is difficult to obtain.

The noise is hard to block out. The modern world is a noisy place. And what makes the noise of today so invasive is that it is personal. It is loud, and it is aimed directly at each of us. Don Delillo gave us his novel *White Noise* back in 1985. Even then—before the World Wide Web, smartphones, the technology boom, and all that has come with it—the challenge to humanity of everything being thrown at us in the way of mass commercialism and communication struck a troubling chord.

Today, we have *White Noise* on steroids. It is no longer just murmuring in the background, annoying but bearable and seemingly within our power to easily shut off. No, modern white noise attacks us on a personal level. Your smartphone, if not literally plugged into your body with earphones or a smart watch, then at the minimum spends a good part of the day in your hand and close by your side. Phone calls, texts, WhatsApp messages, Facebook messages, and so on. The list goes on, with the overwhelming amount of communications you receive and, when not receiving, monitor, sometimes literally for those 24 hours and 7 days. And then there is the barrage we all get from the people and the politicians and the marketers of various kinds, as well as others who think they know—because they have access to much of the information on our smartphones.

Where to escape? With conversation, real conversation—but also into silence.

Yet the escape must be permanent. Delillo's *White Noise* warned of what was going wrong with society—in this case, back in 1985 and specifically American society—and the effect of all the noise on communities and families and individuals. There must be a change in the way we live, in the way we construct our societies. Conversation and silence need to be part of our daily lives—and an integral part. They are not an escape, the focus of a retreat in the mountains or daily meditation or prayer. They are life itself.

12

Don't Overthink It

*My idea of good company is the company
of clever, well-informed people
who have a great deal of conversation;
that is what I call good company.*
                                                    —Jane Austen

WE BOTH LOVE to read. How much one reads and likes to read depends on many factors, but the most basic of them all is time. There are no shortcuts when it comes to reading. Yes, some people read faster than others, and there are all sorts of methods you can pick up on your own or from instructors about how to speed up your reading. Yet at the end of the day, reading will always remain a time commitment, and you are left with the choice of whether to make it or not.

Conversation is the same. There are no shortcuts. Indeed, while you may be able to speed up your reading, there is no equivalent in conversation. It seems perhaps as if the more you "advance" in conversation, the more time is required. As you learn to appreciate conversation, as it has become a more important part of your life and you want more of it, the only way to do so is to commit more time. You can't outsource conversation. There's no room for delegation. You can't speed it up. It is yours, and that means you must give up some of your private time if you want to pursue it.

It's not such an easy choice to make in our ever more demanding world. We need to make a living to support ourselves and our families. Work in itself can easily become the single dominant time consumer in one's life. That is particularly so in a world of smartphones that keep us constantly connected to our desks (if we even have desks). It is difficult, and some bosses make it literally impossible, to escape the barrage of work emails and phone calls that can come at all hours of the day and night. In your authors' case, we fall in the category of folks having customers and projects in various time zones around the world. The communications we receive literally 24/7 are sometime urgent. The excuse of "I was out of the office" no longer applies because everyone knows you are always with your phone, so there's no reason you aren't seeing your messages and calls. At best, you are sadly left only with the excuse "I was sleeping." In such scenarios, the connected world quickly transforms into the suffocating world. There would appear to be no escape. Work—and not even just work but other "commitments"—seems inescapable.

We all live with this challenge of carving out time in our lives for things we think are important. The problem with activities like reading and conversation is that they are harder to justify as pursuits to spend your time on. Time for family, the wife or husband or kids, that's an easy one. For exercise, no one is going to say that it's a waste of time. Yet when it comes to so-called pursuits of leisure, society makes things difficult. The real difficulties arise when those pursuits of leisure are seen as having little or no benefit to society. Shopping, in the hierarchy of acceptable leisure activities, places high. Finding time to go shopping is not only seen as positive, but leisure time (especially weekends and holidays) is specifically structured to permit the maximum amount of buying. You don't have to be a cynic to see how Christmas has been overshadowed by Black Friday and Cyber Monday. The biggest impression left on many by the annual celebration of the birth of the Messiah is bargain shopping. There is more interest in sales numbers than in the number of churchgoers. (And it's no surprise that the former is skyrocketing and the latter, dwindling.)

Time is money. This has been ingrained in us as a truism, but, of course, it is completely false. Time is many things, and it's best if we leave it to the physicists and perhaps also philosophers to give their definitions. But you can take our word for it that money won't be in either of their definitions. And whoever is trying to push on you the truism that time is money is probably wasting both your time and your money.

Time is life. That just might be a better way of putting it. From the moment we are born until the moment we die, somewhere in the background the clock is ticking. We, for the most part, can't hear it—or is it that we are simply not listening? As it gets louder—when we grow older or something happens that startles us into the realization that our time is limited and passing—we are awakened to its sound. But for the most part, we are in denial.

So when life provides you with those precious moments when you have toiled enough to feed yourself and your loved ones, lift up your head and breathe deep. There is a beautiful world to discover. And leisure is not a synonym for spending. Society may demand of you a life of consumption and purchasing, but don't buy it (pun intended). That's not what life is really about. Choose the walk in the park or down the city street, the good movie, maybe a bike ride, a trip to the library to pick out a book to read, or, of course, a conversation. Certainly, pursuits of the mind have no intrinsic priority over those of the body. The pleasure in holding your lover's hand can be just as uplifting and enlightening as any intellectual pursuit. It is not the one or the other that is needed. It is both. It is both in their purest and most honest sense.

Reading can put you to sleep—and not just reading at bedtime. It is not easy to maintain your concentration. You encounter words and concepts you at first don't understand. You re-read and still don't get it, but you read on. And then perhaps it happens. Your mind is opened to places and ideas and emotions and people and times, some that seem warm and familiar, others far away and new. You grow, you learn, and you expand your horizons. There would appear to be no limits. Books offer an infinitely large world to explore. We discover a different way of looking at something. We discover something we never knew. We realize we misunderstood something we had long assumed we knew everything about. Making it all that much more special, we can do this lying on our couch at home, sitting in a coffee shop, or wherever else the light is good enough.

There is, however, something missing. Something calling out to us and preventing us from becoming completely lost in our mind: the Other. We cannot do without it. Take it from a guy you might think would be the first in line for some good spiritual escapism but instead prefers rolling up his sleeves so he can play in the mud that makes up the real world. "If I had been asked in my early youth whether I preferred to have dealings only with men or only with books, my answer would certainly have been in favor of books. In later years, this has become less and less the case," explains Buber.

> Not that I have had so much better experience with men than with books; on the contrary, purely delightful books even now come my way more often than purely delightful men. But the many bad experiences with men have nourished the meadow of my life as the noblest book could not do, and the good experiences have made the earth into a garden for me.

It is not either-or, either the life of the hermit or the life of a socialite; either the life of the intellect or a life of passion. Buber's point is that both are essential, and he wisely points out that while the realms of the mind that make up the intellectual and spiritual sides of humankind can potentially be beautiful and uplifting, they can never ultimately compete with real experience, with life—as dirty and complicated and, yes, even many times evil as our world can be. Buber, a deeply religious man, at the most fundamental level chooses earth over heaven. We must put life first. Indeed, in Buber's world, the way to reach the divine is through open and honest connection with others. Books and learning and education may (or may not) lay the seeds. But ultimately the test is how we interact with fellow human beings.

"Reading is an act of contemplation, perhaps the only act in which we allow ourselves to merge with the consciousness of another human being."[33] Well, perhaps *almost* the only. What about talking? No, not talking to yourself, but talking to someone else. Isn't that where there is true potential to "allow ourselves to merge with the consciousness of another human being"? Books can be great. They can be enlightening and intriguing and can open us up to new worlds and ideas. Books can connect us to times and places like no other medium and also to people—in particular, to historical figures. But for real connection in the present, most certainly with those in our immediate vicinity but really with just about anyone, conversation, not reading, provides the answer.

We may read. We may think. We may or may not also dream or pray. We can analyze or deconstruct or critique as well. Yet these will always be first steps. Next must come dialogue. Next must come conversation. That is the path to real understanding and knowledge.

And not only that, but conversation is also a path to peace.

Consider it for a moment. It is easy to discount the argument as "New Age" and unrealistic or, at best, wishful thinking. But try instead to listen for a moment, to look around. Is this wishful thinking or in fact brutal reality? Where there is no conversation, you'll find violence and death and destruction. And today, just about everyone is to blame for this dire situation, the Left as well as the Right. We have inherited a world that is splitting apart, preferring divisions and differences over empathy and understanding. On one side, the advocates of intellectual materialism are confident they will find all the answers in reason and science. On the other

---

[33] David L. Ulin, *The Lost Art of Reading* (Seattle: Sasquat Books, 2010), p. 16.

side, traditionalists hold firm to old and new wave spiritual and tribal impulses. This clash of ideologies appears doomed to destroy humanity in a zero-sum conflict in which all appear destined to be losers.

Conversation offers a way out—not by providing answers but by providing a path. It is a path that continues to require hard thinking and reason, yet of a somewhat different kind than we are familiar with from the classroom or a library or even a research laboratory. Real conversation demands connection and empathy—not just with your friends but also with your enemies. It rejects easy answers. It demands both doubt and understanding, doubt in that everything can be questioned. And though you must continue to think while engaged in conversation, the trick is not to think too much. Let your thoughts flow freely. Try to explain yourself, and, as the dialogue develops, don't hesitate to try to address issues you had not thought about or that perhaps challenge what you were saying. Let your thoughts run free, but also know when to stop them and to listen and reflect. You are not in a debate. You are not defending your thesis or belief or viewpoint. You are in a conversation, where there are no winner and losers, and indeed in which everyone's a winner. Start listening; explore what your partner or partners in conversation are saying; contemplate their ideas; ask questions. Hold your thoughts for later. They aren't important.

There is no question that cannot be asked, no topic that is too sacred to be probed and analyzed. Understanding is required, in the same way that connection and empathy are. Indeed, understanding is what allows for the connection and empathy. We don't mean the type of understanding in which you arrive at and hold your truths and beliefs to be the only correct ones, but the understanding that allows you to see not just the truths you hold dear but also those held by others, even when they stand in contradiction to your own.

No, everyone is not right all the time. Human history is littered with beliefs and ideas that have been proved not just wrong but also dangerous. The challenge is to uproot such ideas with respect and understanding. Show that your counterpart is wrong, not that he or she is stupid. This can only come through dialogue in which all sides first work to understand the other, to listen and question in order to understand what is being said and why. Don't dismiss something in an off-handed manner but attempt to find the kernel of truth that is contained even in the ideas you most reject and despise. This is the path offered by real conversation: a connection with others that is honest and open and willing to explore, void of preconceived prejudices. Only conversation offers this way forward. Solitary intellectual thought can open the door. So can a book, a work of art, a television show, and even a research laboratory. Yet it is only through honest interpersonal connection that dialogue leading to real change can be achieved.

Here is the best proof of what happens in a world without conversation: Just look around at all the hatred and prejudice. Such short memories we have! Only one or two generations ago, our parents or grandparents lived in a world literally at war, with millions killed and mass destruction on nearly every continent. In the wake of World War II, we were initially left believing we had figured it out. Europe—so-called enlightened Europe, which saw itself as the standard-bearer of reason and justice and everything civilized, only to end up as the root cause of the two massive world wars of the last century—saw its borders begin to come down and started to understand that only by putting aside old prejudices and false patriotism could world order be maintained. Yet the hope proved short lived and was built on a false sense of greater understanding between people. The prejudices and hatred were still there—and strong. Shortsighted politicians on both sides of the Atlantic found these feelings fuel for their equally shortsighted agendas and power grabs, but it would be wrong simply to blame them. The problem runs much deeper. The establishments in Washington and Brussels, as well as in other Western capitals, completely misread the landscape. They thought that all was "fine," only to discover later that they had merely been talking to, and listening to, themselves. They were not engaged in real conversation. Rather, they were cooped up in their ivory towers, decked out with beautiful buildings and green grass, where they listened to the soothing sound of their own voices telling them what they already thought they knew and were more than happy to have supported. The acoustics were perfect in the ivory tower.

There was no doubt. There was no listening to the Other. The reasoning and analysis went only far enough in their books and policy papers and minds for them to hear the echo of their own supporting voices. "They" were both liberal and conservative, on the Left and the Right, comprising the established Western political and intellectual orders. What a surprise awaited them!

There was also a second echo chamber at work. From the outset, it rejected listening and believed it had the answers to establish a new and better world order. All people had to do was obey the mandates of the enlightened leadership. A classic example is the Turkey of Kemal Ataturk. His grand modernization program was, on the face of it, a great success. He turned the ruins of the Ottoman Empire into an economic and geopolitical powerhouse. Only, on the way, he first permitted the Armenian genocide and the murder of others who stood in the way of his grand plans, and then he and his political heirs made the same mistake as their friends in Europe and the United States of listening only to themselves—in this example, the political, military, and economic elites of Istanbul and Ankara. Ignored and left behind, the masses of Turks became an easy feeding ground for Islamic fundamentalists who took advantage of the void.

Conversation begins too often where leaders stop. No one wants to be questioned and challenged—perhaps most especially politicians. They, at most, want to play to their so-called constituents, to the home crowd. The political, cultural, and intellectual establishments in the West completely failed their societies at the end of the twentieth century and the start of the twenty-first. They preached openness and inclusiveness. They even tried to legislate it. But implementation was a complete failure. Whole sectors of these societies were ignored and forgotten. Tragically, the void was filled by a new wave of leaders who preferred to feed off the anger of those who were forgotten, instead of actually addressing the issues about which they are rightfully angry. Where real dialogue was not implemented, demagoguery came in its place—demagoguery that is based on talking to people, telling them what to do and think, taking their anger and fueling it further.

The framework for a path out of this mess is there waiting. Real conversation—inclusive, frank, and honest—holds out hope.

And again, as we ask elsewhere, is this possible? Can real conversation play a more central role in our world? As we write this book, pulling together our thoughts on the issue, as well as those of others such as Buber and Freire and Montaigne, there are two reactions. In order, the first is, "Who are we kidding? This is all wishful thinking. The world never has been and never will be a place for the type of real dialogue and conversation we are describing." But then, on second thought, we recall the obvious. We recall why we set out to write this book in the first place. We are two fairly average people of average backgrounds, and we have seen real conversation in practice, starting with ourselves, but also in our many endeavors. Real conversation is not rocket science. Anyone can do it. More important, it does not require anyone to do something that he or she might not naturally do in any event. It does not go against any so-called underlying human trait or characteristic. Who doesn't enjoy a good conversation? The main challenge: remind yourself how enjoyable good conversations can be, and find opportunities to have more of them with a more diverse group whenever possible.

Perhaps the most under-appreciated of human traits is naivete. Indeed, being naive is seen as a weakness, something you should outgrow, and if you don't outgrow it, you will be burned by it as an adult. The naive, the narrative goes, are the prey of salesmen and dirty politicians and everyone in between who is trying to take advantage of them. In this, the widely held, view, *naive* is another word for *stupid*.

Yes, people, including your authors, are at times naive (and stupid). But just as no one would criticize a person for showing empathy, we should also think twice about knocking naivete because, along with empathy and other human traits that on the face of it make us weak and vulnerable, it is instead our strength. We are naive, and we listen. We are naive, and we show caring and concern. We enter a conversation. Yes, we are letting our guard down. If we maintained all of our protective gear all of the time, we'd just as soon lock ourselves in a bomb shelter somewhere, blocked off from the world but safe. Engaging with someone else—in particular, with someone who is "different"—demands opening up and letting down your guard, at least somewhat. That doesn't mean letting yourself get run over or taken advantage of. It does mean opening up the window, even if just a little bit, to see what is happening outside.

Prejudices and preconceived notions will never disappear, but that's not the goal anyway. The immediate goal is simply to take things down a notch, to the point where we can sit down at the same table together with people who are "different" from us, perhaps in the way they look or what they think. Why is that such a big deal? Ponder the question for a moment. It is meant to be a practical question, just as this book is meant to be "practical" in the sense of offering a look at how things are done that makes one consider again the options. Let's push harder: Is it possible that it is not simply "by chance" that conversation and dialogue are not more popular? Could it be that elements in our society actually benefit from less conversation?

Less conversation means less questioning. It also means less listening. It brings with it a world of us versus them, where each of us is pressured to take a side. Whenever conversation ends, disputes largely begin and flourish, and here there are clear winners and losers. Conflict among the masses is also at times of benefit to the ruling elites. A classic example would be certain policies implemented by the British during their relatively short-lived empire years. These "divide and rule" policies helped allow a small island nation to have the bragging rights of the sun never setting on its worldwide empire, by encouraging divisions in the local populations it ruled. In India, for instance, the British helped fuel animosities between Muslims and Hindus; in Palestine, between Jews and Arabs. The policy tool is an old tactic—attributed to the ancient Greeks—that has been attempted by many a leader and country since.

Does that mean that all conflicts in the world are a result of some evil leader or country trying to manipulate the masses? No. This is not the point. To call for more conversation and dialogue in our personal and political lives is not a call for pacifism. Conversation does not "work" and was never meant to "work" to solve all the world's conflicts. It would be silly to ever make such a claim. But the argument against dialogue and conversation—that they are just Utopian thinking that has no application in the real world—must be confronted because it is one of the main attacks used in particular by those who continue to try to use conflicts to their advantage. Conversation is not the answer to the world's problems, just as there is indeed no one answer, no one simple right way forward. Yet conversation can certainly help keep the flames down. When people are speaking—not just to those whom they agree with but to those who think and look differently than they do—it goes a long way toward people finding more peaceful and inclusive ways to address the challenges that face us.

13 *Conversation and Education*

> *No one will ever shine in conversation,*
> *who thinks of saying fine things:*
> *to please, one must say many things*
> *indifferent, and many very bad.*
> —Francis Lockier

*F*REIRE'S DEMAND FOR true dialogue is made to one of the most important sectors of society—that of educators. This is what makes his treatise so powerful, as he shoots directly at the heart of the issue. "This dialogue cannot be reduced to the act of one person's 'depositing' ideas in another. . . . Nor yet is it a hostile, polemical argument between those who are committed . . . to the imposition of their own truth."[34]

If our children are not brought up in an environment of true dialogue, what will become of them when they are grown? This is a political manifesto. When you demand openness in schools, you are in effect demanding it of society as a whole.

---

[34] Paulo Freire, *Pedagogy of the Oppressed*, English edition 1970, Bloomsbury Publishing, New York, 70.

You can't raise freethinking children in the hopes they will later stay silent and complacent within whatever construct society is trying to impose on them. They will think. They will fight. Because that is the way they have been raised—to listen, yes, but also to question and criticize.

Speaking to someone who agrees with everything you say is just boring. Speaking to a know-it-all who just wants to convert you is simply aggravating. What you want is to speak to people who care. They need to care about you; they need to care about the world. They need to sincerely care about everyone, in the sense that they realize that someone who is different (in any way possible) doesn't make him or her any less of a person or less important or less cared for. It's okay to disagree. It's not okay to belittle.

There must be a common ground, no matter how big or small.

A good friend and colleague of ours, the late Pakistani brigadier general Rashid Malek, visited us in Washington in 2007 and, at our request, gave a lecture on Afghanistan to our American board of adviser members. Rashid was a true gentleman. I had been his guest in Karachi a few years earlier, where he put me up at the local officers' club during my stay, and I got to know him and his family quite well. Rashid had been helping us at that time on a complex multi-million-dollar insurance fraud case that turned out to be part of a larger U.S. government investigation into potential terror financing through insurance fraud. We were conducting our investigation for one of the insurance companies.

Rashid loved his country. He recognized the problems but also the potential. He had served for decades in Pakistan's military. He spent a short stint at West Point, in a U.S.

government program aimed at strengthening ties with the Pakistani military. He was a devout Muslim. He was an adviser to Pakistani presidents. He was a successful businessman, recognized as such both at home and abroad. His clients included leading companies from around the globe—literally from the Americas to Asia.

When we met him, Rashid was an avid tennis player. In his youth, at well over six feet tall, he had played on Pakistan's national basketball team. He recalled when the U.S. basketball star Ferdinand Lewis Alcindor Jr., who later converted to Islam and changed his name to Kareem Abdul-Jabbar, came to visit Pakistan, and Rashid was asked to give him a tour of Karachi. "I had a very small car in those days. He could barely fit in."

Rashid epitomized the complexities of his country and the world. It is so easy to place people into simple groupings but so incorrect. Rashid was secular and religious, a military man and a patriot but also open to criticizing his country for its failings. And as much as he loved and respected the West, he also felt it, too, was fair game for his criticism.

Rashid did not hold back. For well over an hour, he laid out his analysis of the situation in Afghanistan and the "great game" being played out there, which was also spilling over into Pakistan. He ripped into the U.S. government, detailing what he saw as repeated failures in its handling of the Taliban and al-Qaeda in Afghanistan, as well as the United States' policies in Pakistan.

Among those listening were several of our board members who had previously worked for the U.S. government and had even been involved in implementing the very policies Rashid was addressing. Rashid recognized this, but that did not stop him—nor did it stop the Americans from strongly but politely pushing back.

The lecture ended, but the conversation continued late into the night, as the group adjourned to dinner in a nearby restaurant. At times, voices become raised because they all took their work for the government seriously and personally. At other times, the conversation turned to a whisper, as they mentioned names and events not yet known about by the public. These men had operated at the level of both decision makers and operators in the field. They were patriots of the real kind; while defending their country on some points, they were still open to hearing about and understanding the alleged failures.

Between both sides, there was much "common ground." We definitely won't use "love of humanity." These were the kind of guys who didn't like to use expressions that showed weakness or over-sensitivity. Let's just say that while there may not have been a lot of love around that table, there was much understanding. And isn't that what we need more of? Agreement really doesn't get us anywhere. At best, we are left where we stood. No progress. No further consideration that could allow us to advance things. If we all agree, there are no more tough questions. That just brings stagnancy and boring conversations.

We want, again to use Freire's term, *transformation*. We want our conversations to go somewhere or to take us somewhere. "Yes, I agree completely." "Yeah, that's exactly my point of view." "It's crazy how everyone doesn't think just like us." Agreement is a dead end. If the "dead end" were some ultimate Truth, then perhaps we could suffer it. Agreement would mean "Enlightenment" and "True Understanding." The problem is that if you are not a religious fanatic of some kind or another, you realize that at least in the realm of ideas, there is no such last word to which we all must bow down and say, "Amen." Even from a purely materialist perspective, the Truth still evades us. Yes, science has figured things out, many things. But in most cases, when we've figured out one big question, it leads to more. The building blocks of not just our planet but also of the universe were discovered by the great chemists of the eighteenth and nineteenth centuries and neatly displayed in the Periodic Table. But the physicists and the astrophysicists of the late nineteenth century and twentieth centuries calculated that actually "dark matter" made up most (more than 80 percent) of our universe.

We aren't belittling, in any sense, the findings of science and the fact that in many ways they are the closest we have today to "truths." We only use the extreme example of science to raise doubts about any so-called Truths being claimed by priests, philosophers, or politicians—or, for that matter, businessmen, economists, lawyers, and others who claim to have figured it out and, what's even worse, try to force you to accept what they think they've figured out.

The End of History and The Last Man and *The End of Science: Facing the Limits of Knowledge in the Twilight of the Scientific Age* have already been written, actually now more than two decades ago (in 1992 and 1996, respectively). And while they may be interesting reads, the authors basically got it wrong: a lot of groundbreaking history and science have happened since.

Don't believe the experts—we live by that motto. Listen to what they have to say, yes. But listen critically. Discuss critically. And then see what holds water.

And yes, let's take some credit here: a lot of advancements in thought and science come in part to conversations. People, really smart people, who are still smart enough to have doubts in their own certainty about things, continue to talk and explore and dialogue—and not just with like-minded people, but with people who think differently than they do.

BILL: THE DELINQUENT'S TALE

Teenagers do stupid things. That's just part of life in an adult or soon-to-be-adult body but with brains and hormones not fully developed (or reined in?) just yet.

So when a few friends and I got the brilliant idea for our high school senior prank to put dead fish in the principal's office, the possible consequences never occurred to us.

But I suppose that is one of the fun things about being a kid.

So off we drove to the fish market and filled the trunk of my car with a couple of bags of fish.

We realized that fish smelled, but one of the many things we didn't taken into account was just how bad they smelled after sitting in the trunk of a car for hours on a warm spring day in Washington, D.C. Let's just say that it wasn't fun driving around in that car after we picked up the fish.

It was around 10 p.m. that same evening when we headed back to school to carry out the "prank." In retrospect, we do sound like some pretty stupid kids. I think back on our prying open a window to the school and climbing inside with the bags of dead, smelly fish in tow. Getting charged with "breaking and entering" didn't cross our minds. Maybe an alarm would go off, and the police would arrive and accidentally shoot one of us—that wasn't even a consideration. So off we went down the dark high school corridor, making our way to the principal's office, where we deposited the stinking fish.

We thought we had gotten away with it.

The next day we learned otherwise. We were quite proud at first about all the commotion we had caused at school when our senior prank was discovered the next morning. But it only took a couple of hours until one of our gang—myself, that is—was caught. I was called into the principal's office. He had gotten word that my car stank of dead fish. I had been caught red-handed, and when confronted with the fact, I quickly gave myself up. Yes, I did it. It was just supposed to be a joke. No, we hadn't thought much about the fact that we broke into the school and created a complete mess of the principal's office. No, we didn't know the principal was receiving that morning a delegation from China that had come to see firsthand how things work at an American high school. (I wonder whether in China they also have high school pranks.)

"Who did the prank with you?" the principal asked. I'm not really sure why I refused to say. It just seemed like the right thing to do, not to turn in your friends. I was sent home, indefinitely. Other teachers, teachers whom I knew well and respected, also tried to get me to give up my friends. I wouldn't budge.

The principal called me and asked me to come over to his home after school (I was still expelled) so we could speak. I remember the scene quite well, even after all of these years. The principal lived in a small house on the outskirts of the city. We sat in the backyard. He did most of the speaking, trying to pry out of me the names of my cohorts. He ran some names by me—mainly the "usual suspects," guys he knew I hung out with and who had reputations that fit the profile he had put together of who would have been involved. He got it wrong. But he never knew because I continued to refuse to cooperate. He then tried a different tactic, explaining how as a community we needed to be responsible for one another and trust one another, and how my refusal to cooperate was undermining that community.

I didn't say much. My mind was made up. His mind was made up.

Conversations can also be missed opportunities.

Here we had a tremendous opportunity. A pupil sitting and talking with a principal he actually respected and at a school he actually liked attending. There were many great teachers I still remember decades later, teachers who challenged their pupils and opened up their eyes to new ideas and experiences. The school was a center of liberal thought in a very conservative town. Openness and inclusion were its trademarks. It still had a hippy feel about it—no bells between classes, you could leave campus during the day if you didn't have classes, and political activism was encouraged. I fell in love with learning during my high school years, and nearly all of that learning was positive.

But in the end, what I remember is the lost opportunity. Instead of conversation, there was scolding. We need to be clear here: Punishment, fine. There are consequences to our actions, and one of them is that society has rules, and if you break them, you pay. Otherwise, everything breaks down. You broke into school; you are expelled. Fine. But what do you learn from your mistakes? In the fish prank case, you learn that the people you hold as authority, whom you respect for their wisdom and thoughtfulness, can also get it wrong—which is actually an important lesson (though clearly not the one the school was trying to get across).

My principal, sadly, had opted for what Freire described as the "banking" view of education, whereby the teacher/principal is the authority who is depositing knowledge/rules/codes of behavior/and so on, into the pupil, who is simply an "account" receiving deposits. Freire even goes so far as to say there is no real learning in the banking concept of the teacher-pupil relationship. Rather, he argues, only through true dialogue can there be true learning.

At face value, this incident had no grand political implications, and at the most basic level it was just an example of sophomoric behavior by a stupid high school kid. The missed opportunity in my personal fish incident case, however, was that it occurred at a Quaker school, which held itself up to being a bastion of dialogue and openness. Kids in Washington, D.C., at my school in the 1980s might not have found the Quakers' strident pacifism and conscientious objection immediately relevant. But with weekly "silent meetings," at which all were given an equal opportunity, pupils and faculty alike, to stand up and say what was on their minds, and an overall liberal atmosphere, one would have expected a somewhat different reaction. But now that I am older and look back at my "liberal education" and at least some of the liberal circles I lived in at the time and what has ensued since, I can't help but think that so-called liberals, at the end of the day, could be just as good advocates for closed-mindedness as the so-called conservatives they liked to bash.

14

Now You're Making Me Angry

*None of us can ever express the
exact measure of his needs or
his thoughts or his sorrows;
and human speech is like a cracked
kettle on which we tap crude
rhythms for bears to dance to,
while we long to make music
that will melt the stars.*
— Gustave Flaubert,
Madame Bovary

THERE ARE DIFFICULT conversations, signaled by the mere invitation to a discussion. "We have to talk" rarely ends well. Neither does "Could we have a word in my office?" Here the pleasure lies not in the conversation itself, but in its ending— unless that ending is "I want a divorce" or "You're fired!" It could be argued that these are not genuine conversations. Nothing kills a chat like coercion, when one of the parties is dragged into the conversation kicking and screaming.

Such noise is also a feature of the angry conversation. This is a version of the art that has been well noted in the past. Historians have recorded that on the two occasions when Benjamin Franklin met his son William in the summer of 1775, "their conversation ended in shouting matches loud enough to disturb the neighbors." (William was a pro-British loyalist, Ben an American patriot.) Since the late twentieth century, such shouting matches have been climbing to a crescendo. In this period, hosts of bourgeois dinner parties have pleaded with their guests, "No religion or politics please," to try to keep the chatter civil. In conversation, there is a thin line between "lively" and angry. Some intellectuals gave up on even the possibility of conversation.

> They said that we are all solipsists and that what we say is shaped mainly by subconscious passions or by ideas that enter our psyche subliminally. "There is no such thing as conversation," the novelist and essayist Rebecca West argues. "It is an illusion. There are intersecting monologues, that is all." Writing about the novelist and playwright Michael Frayn, a contemporary critic refers to "the hit-or-miss uncertainty, the artificiality, the baffling complexity of conversation."[35]

---

[35] Stephen Miller, *Conversation: A History of a Declining Art*, Yale University Press, 2006.

Some writers have noted the relationship between angry conversations and the amount of information available to citizens of the modern world. First came books and newspapers, pamphlets and magazines. Radio added its cacophony of voices, then television, and finally, the ubiquitous Internet in our pockets. It is hard to see how the information dump could be augmented any further unless we move to brain implants delivering a never-ending flow of data from an infinite Wi-Fi. Hell at last, and fire and brimstone are a good part of it.

The contribution of increased information to angry conversations would seem illogical. Wasn't this the philosophers' dream—universal access to all the knowledge in the world? Better-educated and -informed citizens would download facts and figures and opinions that would turn every conversation into an informed, delightful debate. If we substitute the word *tribal* for *angry* in the description of many modern conversations, it's a clue to what went wrong. More information has become too much, and, as is obvious from social media on the Internet, there is more than enough of it to divide and subdivide into micro-topics. Each cultural and sub-cultural group is supplied with its own mass of partisan data. Each has a following of passionate, committed and, yes, angry adherents—but not informed. Ill-informed but right is the new norm.

"This is the age of the screed, the rant, the tirade, the jeremiad, the diatribe, the venom-fueled, white-hot harangue!" *Washington Post* columnist Peter Carlson wrote in 2004. Bring a leftist and a rightist or a religious person and an atheist to any conversation, and you have two combatants, each weaponized with an array of facts, opinions, and convictions drawn from his or her social media tribe. That guarantees that each has so much dogma to unload into any debate that delivering it has priority over listening to the other side. "I have all the information and certainty I need; I know all that is false about your side, so just shut up, listen up and learn."

Anyone who has sat down to a dinner table in the twenty-first century with people from differing political, social, or ethnic camps will have experienced the often abrupt switch from jovial conversation to rising voices and angry accusations. The table suddenly is split into warring camps—one is branded as fascist or communist, as a heathen or a superstitious primitive, as a greedy capitalist or a welfare-bum apologist, as a stupid American or a back-stabbing European. The conversation has changed from friendly consensus built on amusing anecdotes to a never-ending stream of "What about" . . ." —cherry-picked facts or myths drawn from the tribal databases. "Our spirits are corroded by living in an atmosphere of unrelenting contention—an argument culture," author Deborah Tannen wrote.[36] Ernest Hemingway's little gem of a short story *Hills Like White Elephants* is about a failure to communicate in a conversation.

A man and "the girl with him" are sitting in a railroad station cafe. Their inconsequential conversation about the landscape they see from their table reveals a certain tension in their relationship. Then we learn that the man wants the woman to have an abortion, though he refers to it only obliquely. He says she should do what she wants to do, but it is clear that he is trying to persuade her to get the abortion. The woman becomes annoyed by the man's unctuous solicitude.

---

[36] Deborah Tannen, *The Argument Culture: Moving from Debate to Dialogue*, Random House, New York (1998).

"Can't we maybe stop talking?" she asks. A few sentences later, she seems on the edge of hysteria. "Would you please please please please please please please stop talking?" The woman is sick of the man's pretended concern for her well-being. After he says something to comfort her, she says, "I'll scream."

Yes, it's going to get dirty, headed for the mud pit or even the septic tank. Conversation is close to being over as people listen only to themselves and want you to agree with how right they are. There is no political discourse. There is name-calling, accusation, shouting, or even violence. There is no listening. It doesn't have to be that way. Here's another story about some friends of ours.

One is an American journalist, now retired, who had a political column for more than ten years on a U.S. newspaper. From the 1970s to the '90s, he knew all the important political people in Washington, D.C., and many across the country. He loves to recall a trip to Arkansas in the 1980s to meet then governor Bill Clinton and Hillary. He had spent the day with the Clintons for a column he was writing. As an old-time journalist, while he was working he kept his political views to himself. Now, he would accept the liberal label.

By contrast, another friend had retired as a decorated Central Intelligence Agency career officer. He had moved from field agent to station chief with assignments in Europe, Asia, and Africa. His politics are conservative. First through our work and later as friends, we have often brought these two together. When the talk is business, it's business. They were at the top of their professions, and we have benefited from their great experience. Work aside, when the conversation turns to contemporary topics, things can get heated. Don't think Donald Trump supporter and Hillary Clinton supporter. Think Barry

Goldwater versus Lyndon Johnson or even Nixon-Kennedy. Our friends' politics could not have been more different. No, neither is going to convert the other at this point in their lives, but neither are their heads in the sand with butts in the air. They know how to articulate their disparate views, but they also know how to really listen, to show empathy. It was part of their jobs to see things from someone else's perspective. From that, they learned to grow by holding dialogue with people different from themselves.

One evening we were dining with these two and some other friends at a favorite spot outside Washington. They were sitting next to each other at one end of the table. At some point late in the evening, they were speaking quietly, inaudible to the rest of the table. We took note and tried to tune in to bits of their conversation. In his youth, our journalist friend had been a political activist in what was then labeled a far-left group. Our CIA friend, working for the government, was busy infiltrating the same group at the same time. During recent years, we had heard our friends arguing about many topics, one as a classic leftist, the other from the right. The conversations were often heated and emotional. Both cited firsthand experience. One had the knowledge of a Washington media insider, the other that of an intelligence gatherer around the world. They had watched history unfold in the final, end-of-history quarter of the twentieth century. There had been Vietnam and Iraq, Watergate and Whitewater, the good and the evil in American domestic and foreign policies. They had strong opinions, and they knew how to articulate them; they had direct knowledge to drive their points home.

For fans of classic conversation, it was a joy to watch, an education to listen to them talk. What an honor to be part of such a conversation! For all the information and wit, the real beauty of their conversation was not their ability to argue. It was their willingness to listen. Their worlds could not be more opposite. One was a fighter, who had spent much of his life overseas; the other, a writer, roamed Washington, D.C., and rarely traveled abroad. In these different perspectives, there was little agreement, and yet there was a bond and mutual understanding. Each did not bunker down in his own foxhole. There was opening up and acceptance; each learned from the other.

Real conversation used to be about learning, about sharing, not convincing. You listen and you grow. You engage as yourself, confident in who you are and what you believe, not defensive. You are strong in your beliefs but do not believe you know it all.

Doubt has a bad name. Be confident in your truth; that's what makes a real person. Hold on to your traditions and knowledge. Of course, you don't know everything—that's why we invented school, university, and scientific research, so we can learn more. That's all fine and acceptable to explore, on condition it's on so-called firm ground.

What is not up for discussion is faith-based belief. In politics, religion, cultural norms, and even our explanations of the world around us, the tribe knows best. There is no room for doubt. There is no need for a real conversation about it. We know it all.

Know-it-alls are a dangerous majority in the world and aren't interested in conversation. Their mission is to preach, not to listen, not to learn. For social exchange, there is the illusion of conversation with like-minded know-it-alls. There are the same hymn sheets to sing from in the echo chamber. If you want a vision of the future, imagine Fox News stamping on a human ear forever.

Is it unfair to be critical of the human urge to tribalize? It was once essential for survival, but isn't it time to toss the tribe in the trashcan of evolution? Granted, it's still natural for humans to hang out with those who are like themselves—ethnic groups, religious groups, even class groups. But what is a modern tribe anyway? We once heard a Sri Lankan airline pilot admit that he felt nothing in common with his countrymen when he went home. Vacations were a bore. "My tribe is people who fly airplanes," he said. "I love being at hotels and events with international pilots and aircrew. It's my world; we speak the same language."

He's right. In an ever-changing world, our places are changing. Over millions of years, humans evolved in environments of imperceptible change. Now they struggle to keep up with changes beyond individual control. They are like the desperate polar bears learning to forage in urban trashcans as their habitat melts around them. Who knows what it means for their young and their communities in the future?

A little ahead of the bears, we, too, are individuals, but also families, societies, towns, and cities. And still, we are animals with primal survival instincts. If we don't adapt, we will die, and it looks likely we'll take the whole planet with us.

We still look to ancient Athens to see how democracy and cultural norms evolved that became the basis of Western civilization. Could we apply the political structure of Pericles to the modern world? Absurd. Athens was a tiny entity that had tenuous alliances with nearby city-states in unpopulated small territories.

Our ideal today could not be small societies of like-minded elite men (who exclude women). As Alexander the Great expanded Greek culture eastward, it was not Athenian democracy that he established. It was Persian despotism.

In our interconnected global society, elitist tribal nationalism is suicide for the planet. Openness is the only way forward, and conversation is one of the tools. Joining a conversation doesn't mean giving up who you are and what you know and love. Without You, there is no conversation; neither is there one without the Other. The aim of dialogue is not for one to give up, but for both to open up.

British writer Karen Armstrong believes Western societies are failing to listen to the views of others. In *The Bible, a Biography*, she examines how Hebrew and Christian texts were perceived in ancient times. She argues that the ancients were far more open to interpreting religious texts. Bigoted intransigence on religious topics is a modern phenomenon, she writes. Now, religion fuels bloodshed and conflict, instead of love and understanding. If we want to understand one another, one has to assume the other is speaking the truth. Logician N. L. Wilson believes critics must apply the principle of charity to interpreting alien texts. They must do so in light of the known facts and maximize truth among the sentences of the corpus.

The linguist Donald Davidson concurs. "Making sense of the utterance and behavior of others, even at their most aberrant, requires you to find a great deal of truth and reason in them. Their beliefs may be very different from your own but you have to assume that the alien is very much the same as you. Otherwise, you are in danger of denying their humanity." Davidson says charity is forced upon us. Whether we like it or not, if we want to understand others, we must regard them as right in most matters. Yet in the public arena, people are often presumed to be wrong before they prove to be right.[37]

Armstrong is a religious apologist. She searches for a defense of the spiritual that comes from all the world's religions. We are not taking one side or another in the debate on religion, but you might catch us some evening in a furious debate on the topic. What we borrow from her is her assertion that the only way forward is through understanding. If we want to understand another person, we have to assume that he or she is speaking the truth.

That is a root of real conversation—understanding, in all its meanings. In conversations, we connect with others. We see one another's concerns and passions; we can learn. We can put ourselves at ease, in empathy with others, and see what they can show us that we have missed. Greater understanding is a beautiful thing. It's not a beauty that's ornamental. It's something our world cannot do without.

Religion is the topic that people avoid most if they are around those with different beliefs and views. Politics comes a close second in this divisive era. Having a conversation on these topics may seem both a non-starter and a dead end. How sad. There should be nothing more interesting than a good conversation about whether or not God exists, nationalism is a savior or a Satan, or Europe is best as separate states or a union. What are we left to talk about: the weather? The weekend football match? . . . God help us.

The problem is not the extremists. They can be tolerated. Let them believe that the earth is flat or was created just over

---

[37] Karen Armstrong, *The Bible, a Biography*, Grove Press, New York, 2007, p. 227.

five thousand years ago. Let them preach hatred and even racism and chauvinism. They can be beaten back by reason and understanding—not on every occasion, not in every battle, but in the war. Reason will prevail. Yet there is a condition, a big condition: we can't castrate Reason. We can't raise children who aren't curious and willing and able to ask hard questions of themselves and their world. We can't as adults accept an atmosphere where extreme opinions not only prevail, but we refuse to put them to the test on grounds they are "too holy" or "too sacred." Everything must be open for discussion. Conversation must be encouraged—yes, even between persons of different opinions. There must be respect for the Other. Only then, on a level playing field, does reason have a chance. That means real conversation must not just be tolerated but encouraged—real conversation both as free and open dialogue and as honest, unprejudiced encounter. Only then will the barriers of ignorance crumble. Fear not the haters or even the inexperienced or the "uneducated."

What we must fear and fight against are those who refuse to engage with others, building physical, social, and psychological barriers between individuals, communities, and nations. Barriers and man-made divisions are tools of oppression. The British were experts at it in the short-lived days of their empire. Divide and rule, from Palestine to India to China—wherever the British flag hung—was their method of ensuring control of their territories. To allow, for instance, the Jews and the Muslims in Palestine or Hindus, Sikhs, and Muslims in India to try to work together would have meant an even quicker end to colonial rule. Instead, the British inflamed hatred and undermined conversation between the various ethnic and religious groups within the states they ruled. The damage they did still plays out today. An atmosphere of hatred and closed-mindedness is easy to encourage and painfully difficult to reclaim or maintain. Conversation is always an easy target to attack and undermine and a great challenge to nurture and spread.

15

The Business of Conversation

Travel, instead of broadening the mind,
often merely lengthens the conversation.
—Elizabeth Drew

ENERAL CONSTANTINOS ACHILLIDES. His name alone brings on a feeling of power and respect. So did the first brief description we were given of him, prior to flying from London to Larnaca to meet with him: retired Greek general, Cypriot guerrilla leader in the island's War of Independence against occupying British forces, former head of the Republic of Cyprus Central Intelligence Service or KYP. We were introduced to the general when we worked for a London-based private security and intelligence company. The firm was looking to open up a regional office and thought of partnering with General Achillides, who himself had just retired from government service and set up a private security company in the Cyprus capital, Nicosia. One of the partners at our London firm, ex-MI6, had known the general when he headed his country's intelligence service. So a meeting was arranged at his new company's offices in Nicosia.

Thus began a new conversation in our lives, a conversation that has grown and blossomed for more than two decades. Dialogue and encounter. Business, yes—but also friendship. Possible? Yes, if adequate proof is the reality of what transpired: Connection that transcends the material. Discussions of life and love, philosophy (of course, Greek, but not exclusively), along with business deals and client development.

General Achillides' office was on the second floor of an old Nicosia colonial period home that had been converted into an office. The building stood on one of the city's main roads, Kennedy Avenue, a block down from the ultra-modern and massive Cyprus Central Bank building. Nicosia was and is a small sleepy capital city. On the surface, all is quiet, as if nothing much is going on. Underneath lie the fabled vaults of the Central Bank that hold the secret to how this unassuming eastern Mediterranean island has profited from the problems of its neighbors. First came the wealthy from nearby Lebanon (just a thirty-minute flight) and other Arab states. Next the rich of the warring Balkan states found refuge, later followed by oligarchs from Eastern Europe and Russia. The sleepy island of Cyprus became the safest place to hide their money.

At our first meeting, General Constantinos Achillides immediately became "Kostas," the shortened form of his first name (though his Greek friends call him Takis). The meeting itself was rather short. We had arrived around noontime. Kostas insisted on taking us to lunch. He drove us to an unpretentious fish *taverna* on the outskirts of the city. "You can leave your things in the car. Nothing to worry about. I don't even need to lock the doors," Kostas explained. The restaurant owner and Kostas exchanged greetings. We were shown to a table, but no sooner had we sat down than Kostas got up and told us to follow him as he headed to the restaurant kitchen. In a large industrial-size refrigerator, partially hidden by ice, was an array of fresh fish for our choosing. We left it to our new friend to decide what looked best, and we headed back to our table, but not before the fish he had chosen was weighed by the owner and taken to be cooked.

A colorful meze was soon laid out in front of us, and first ouzo (with ice and water) and then local white wine were brought to the table. We were in for a feast. It was the first of many with our new friend and soon to also be business partner. The conversation flowed as freely as the wine, and the simple but fresh and plentiful food filled our stomachs and warmed our souls. Time passed. It was as if we'd forgotten our purpose for being there. Had we been deceived? Was this all just a ploy by the Greek general to take advantage of a naive American and Irishman? He did such a good job, it might appear, that we didn't even notice we were being played. In fact, however, we didn't notice because we weren't being played.

The transition from mundane to sublime was seamless. It passed unnoticed. We had just met a few hours ago, total strangers. We were already behaving like old friends. Lunch was finished, the wine bottle empty. Yet there was still time for good strong Cyprus coffee and sweets. No one was thinking about the time. We were simply enjoying the moment, unaware on one level of what was transpiring, but on another, we felt our mood or spirit or soul, whatever you fancy to call it, uplifted.

At some point we returned to the office. We had work to do, phone calls to make, and emails to send. Some of what we had to do was interesting—for instance, analyze and put together strategies to pursue security and intel projects in the regions, such as security for embassies and oil pipelines. We also devised ways to gather intel on a range of topics of interest to our clients from the position of the major players in an upcoming OPEC meeting on the stability of certain regimes in the region. Other topics were a complete bore, such as figuring out margins on a proposed small local guard project. It was all in a day's work.

Later, Kostas invited us to his home. For security reasons, he continued to live in a house in the government compound just behind the Foreign Ministry in Nicosia. It was an older two-story structure—not fancy at all, but with a warm and cozy feel. We sat outside on plastic chairs around a card table that quickly filled up with beer bottles and glasses and an array of nuts and fruit. It was a warm summer day, and as the sun set, we enjoyed the cool breeze that provided relief from the day's heat and the conversation that rambled on into the night.

THOMAS: THE TRAVEL-HATER'S TALE

Our business intelligence company has a small staff and every year we pay for a non-working retreat for them in some venue of their choice. In 2017, it was Istanbul. We were in a seafront cafe with our old friend Kostas, the retired Greek general from Cyprus, musing about travel:

Bill: Kostas, your wife was telling us she's never been to Paris, and you don't want to go. What's the matter with you? My grandmother, up to her last days, was traveling the world. She would take a ship and go to Africa or India...
Kostas: Who was paying?
Bill: She'd had several husbands who left her money.

Thomas: So she took them on cruises and threw them overboard?

[Laughs all round]

Bill: That's why you're wrong, Kostas. That's the most beautiful thing in the world. You have to take your wife to Paris.

Kostas: No. Why?

Bill: Can you believe a man who doesn't want to take his wife to Paris? She's never been!

Kostas: You have to remember that in life, things happen in time, in place, and with means.

Thomas: Yes, and so?

Kostas: The time of the human being is from 0 to 90. Let's say that, because I plan to go to 90.

Bill: Why not 120?

Kostas: I think Bill Clinton said, "Before I die, the average life span will reach 120." But anyway, for now, I plan for 90. Being at the point I am now – 78 – and counting up the means I need, and being in Cyprus, I can make a good life for such a person as my wife. If I want to push time back and try to act as if I am 50, then I need more strength and money and means. But I am not 50. Everybody must act in accord with their time and place and means.

Bill: I don't understand what you're saying. You can't afford to go to India, so then you won't go to India.

Kostas: I could say no simply because I don't know what would be the outcome of my visit.

Bill: I saw your wife today walking around Hagia Sophia. Now obviously I don't know her so well, but it seemed to me she was in heaven – excited, interested and engaged. That is wonderful.

Kostas: And what is the use of that?

Thomas: Well, you're just a lousy tourist.

[Laughter]

Bill: You're so close-minded. But if you open your mind, travel is the most wonderful thing in the world. You meet new people, learn to appreciate new cultures. One thing I really like about my work is the travel – to me traveling is a marvelous thing.

Kostas: Anyway, that is a special thing only for one human being, because everyone is different. I have a good friend who is a doctor, my age, and one day he said to me we should go on a trip to Paphos. I said, why? He said, "there are some good plots near the sea. We should go see them and maybe buy something." I said, why? He said, "because we can make money; the prices will go up for sure." I told him, I think you should go there yourself and buy a tomb – then they'll have somewhere to put you when you die.[38] It's the only thing you need at your age. If you want me to go with you to Paphos, to go to a nice restaurant, to have a good meal and drink wine and enjoy ourselves with our wives, let's go. But not for this reason.

Bill: So, for the same reason, you could go to India to have good meals and enjoy the beautiful views. Same goes for Paris ...

---

[38] Paphos is famous for ancient rock-carved Tombs of the Kings along its Mediterranean coastline. Kostas was suggesting his friend buy one of them.

Kostas: I don't need it. I can have a good time in Cyprus.

Bill: And Paris is closer. There's an idea – next year we could take the staff on the annual retreat to Paris. It's easy to get Paris, and it's closer and more doable than Venice, which they're suggesting. And it's probably cheaper.

Thomas: Ouch! I don't think so. I doubt that Paris is cheaper than Venice.

Bill: Well, we usually go in September-October. That would make your wife happy, Kostas and that's the most important thing.

Kostas: What about making me happy?

Bill: Not you. We're not going to listen to you. We'll listen to your wife and go to Paris.

Kostas: I want you to plan for the retreat at my village house in Tera in Cyprus next year.

[Laughter]

Bill: Maybe the year after ...

Thomas: Or the next year after; or the year after that.

[Afterword: The following summer, Kostas took his wife on a driving holiday in the south of France. And on to Paris. For the next annual retreat, we took the staff to Lisbon.]

* * * * * *

We have a problem that you may have already picked up on. On one hand, we set a high ideal for true conversation: Honest, open, and uplifting. A merging of dialogue and encounter that touches on the spiritual. Sounds easier said than done. Maybe even impossible?

On the other hand, maybe it isn't that difficult. Many of us are lucky enough to have a few close friends, people it's fun and easy to be with, whom it's great talking with. And throw in some good food and alcohol, an exotic location or two, and doesn't that leave us with a recipe for true conversation we can all handle?

If it were only so easy, we could all have it. And if it were only so impossible, we could just dismiss it. But in fact it's neither and both. And we are now going to make it even more complicated.

Actually, on second thought, we are going to make it easier—and probably on some level less interesting.

One of the characteristics we listed earlier of real conversations is "educational." We explained that through conversation, we "learn, expand our horizons, and even open ourselves up to new experiences in the course of real conversations. That person we are speaking with, whoever he or she may be, can show us so much, and we have so much we can offer, if only we open ourselves up to a true conversation."

Conversation helps us figure things out. We appear to be contradicting ourselves. Indeed, we appear to be saying something that completely undercuts one of our fundamental arguments: that real conversations at their root are about process and not about ends—in particular, not of purely proactive purpose. We want conversations that create bonds between people, that help us grow personally. We aren't here suggesting a better way for people to get things done or to make money.

So, how can we now go on to say that conversation is good for business?

For starters, because that is what we've seen and experienced in our own lives as people engaged in real conversation for three decades, a good part of which were with colleagues.

But before we talk about our experiences, let's return to Xenophon, the ancient Greek philosopher-general who was an advocate of conversation and alcohol. After a long day of battle, relaxation was in order. Food and drink were requirements for that, as well as good conversation with your comrades. The day's battle wasn't going to be your first choice of topics. You wanted to get your mind off that, so talk focused on family and loved ones and political developments and whatever topic gave relief from the troubles and difficulties of the previous hours. The drinking and eating might continue late into the night. Things would inevitably return to the immediate issues of the day, at times even specific battle plans for the next morning. It was in this atmosphere—often drunken, certainly loud—that Xenophon concluded that at times good ideas were developed. Of course, with his caution: check the "brilliant" idea in the morning, when you are sober, before proceeding to adopt it.

Talking things through works. This should come as no surprise. If, as we argued earlier, real conversation is a tool of free thinking, a mechanism through which we develop and test our thoughts, there should be no limits to its applications. So we need real conversation in our personal lives (i.e ., in talking with our friends and acquaintances and decision making as relates to our own lives), in our studies and our research (no matter what the field), and also at work. You must talk things through if you are going to be able to figure them out. You must be able to articulate and defend what you have decided. It's fine to think of something yourself, but the only way you will know if it has any value is by putting it to the test, at least initially through conversation and discussion.

In a business, the usual way to "talk things through" is at a meeting. It can be just the two of you or can be held around a large conference table, maybe even with a couple of additional people on a conference call line who are also made part of the meeting. Now, for those of us who have sat through such meetings, we can attest to the fact that oftentimes the meetings are just a waste of time. Lot of talking, some note taking, but is nothing resolved, nothing is figured out. Not in all cases, of course, but in many. And the conversation around the office conference table is particularly ineffective when the issues are tough.

Reason: The conversation is not an honest one.

And why should it be? It is just a conversation if that is how you enter into it. Indeed most, if not all, of our conversations have a practical purpose. They are aimed at a goal, at getting something done, at deciding whether or not to proceed with the deal, at convincing our boss we deserve a raise, or impressing our boss with how smart we are, so that when she's deciding on staff raises, our name is at the top of the list. So, for the most part, those conversations around the conference room table aren't honest conversations.

It is not a given that the conversation around the conference room table is not an honest one. Nevertheless, we wouldn't expect the type of honesty at the office that we arrive at even with close friends only occasionally. We may not be (and why would we have to be?) friends with a particular colleague or boss. But why all of tension? Why do some people at the table feel too intimidated to offer their opinions? Why do others rush to support the senior person even though they might not completely agree with her? Why so much silence?

We have our opinions on the topic, but we'll leave it to the experts to figure it out. Reams have been written and reams more will be written about how companies, large and small, make decisions. The experts have made giving advice on how to make business decisions—how to run companies, how to run meetings, and so on—a big business in itself.

Our small contribution to the topic is just this: talking works, and when it is real, sincere, honest talking; when you've actually put aside your immediate needs and agendas; and when you are not just thinking of yourself but also of others, you can figure out the so-called tough issues.

So, go tell your boss you've just read a book that is advocating longer coffee and lunch breaks and in general getting staff out of the office as much as possible. We'll also be happy if you use us for an excuse with a spouse or a girlfriend or a boyfriend. "Where were you all afternoon when I was trying to reach you?" "Out to lunch with a friend." "For over two hours and not answering your phone?" "Yes, I just read this book that said having a long lunch with a friend can be good not only for you personally, but also often helps you with work."

In an earlier chapter, we talked about sitting at an upscale Midtown restaurant at 1 p.m. and watching how quickly everyone got through lunch. This was no fast-food joint but featured chef-made Italian cuisine. Yet no one was slowing down to enjoy the food. No one around us had ordered a glass of wine (or, God forbid, an actual bottle of wine to drink with lunch). They had to get back to the office quickly. That's where work was done and real important decisions were made.

Yes, we and our colleagues laughed a little about what we saw, but we were really mainly sad. This was the type of life we were aiming for—the success of working in Midtown Manhattan and rubbing shoulders with the movers and shakers of American, no, world, commerce—and this was what it came down to: a 50-minute max lunch break so you could get back to your desk.

We needed to get out fast to save our sanity.

Not that things are actually "sane" in the lunchtime-world of Nicosia, Cyprus. Actually, we'll leave it to you to judge. We have a wealthy friend in the Cyprus capital who decided that it made sense to set up his own restaurant in the middle of town. Because he was already spending so much time eating out with clients and prospective clients, he figured it was practical to have his own place.

And a great place it is, packed every weekday from 12:30 to 3:30 p.m. with customers, often including our friend himself, having long leisurely lunches. And wine on just about every table. Here and in similar scenes at restaurants throughout the Cyprus capital are where many important conversations take place.

By the way, our friend also owns a winery. When we last visited him at his office, the official meeting was, as always, on the short side, and then it was off to the restaurant for the real conversation. He suggested we try a new rosé from his winery. We usually avoid rosé, as it is normally a little too much on the sweet side for us. But he convinced us to give his winery's rosé a try, and it indeed was excellent, going perfectly with the traditional Greek meze and fish.

Whoever said, "Don't mix business and pleasure"? He or she clearly never had a "business lunch" in Cyprus. And don't get us wrong. Yes, we love the food and the wine and, of course, the break from work. But what we really love is the conversation.

So, get out of the office. Go have a coffee or lunch with a friend—and start talking.

If that friend also happens to be a business partner or colleague, don't make the conversation only about work topics. That would be boring. It is for us. When we are out of the office, we are also looking for a break. The last thing you want to take with you to lunch are the problems from the office. Talk about football or family or friends, even the weather. But take advantage, as we do, of being with a friend. Talk about what's really on your mind, what's bothering you. It can be a personal issue or even something in the news, but when you talk about something you really care about, it shows. It gets your friend to relax and open up, too. She may also take the opportunity to bring up something on her mind or ask you questions or just give you her thoughts about what you have brought up. And the conversation begins to flow. It feels comfortable. It feels good.

If it's a business partner or colleague, the conversation might circle back to a topic related to work. But now that you're both speaking "unofficially," with nothing to lose or gain, the ideas flow more freely. What seemed like an insurmountable obstacle suddenly turns into an opportunity.

Our line of work is primarily intelligence. We are investigators, researchers, and analysts who on a regular basis are being presented with various challenges in getting our clients the information they need to make critical business decisions. One day we may be looking at a mining company in sub-Saharan Africa; the next, we hear from a Russian oligarch who is best friends with the Russian president; and then on Friday afternoon, we get a frantic call from a major U.S. manufacturing company that has just discovered a senior executive might have been taking bribes from its Bangkok-based regional distributor and needs us to figure out what really happened.

Rarely is it an easy job. Often, at least some elements of each project are literally completely new to us. Solving these problems isn't simply about being smart. It's more about thinking creatively and, most important, thinking creatively as a team because none of these projects are one-person shows. Often, we need to send team members into the field, to locations literally around the globe. There are usually no easy approaches.

That's when the brainstorming is needed.

We probably should make it our company's motto: Get creative. Get talking.

Of course, it starts in the office, and you need to get as much input as possible. You can't have a real conversation in business if you don't have some idea of what you are talking about. We hate the term *experts*. You know—the same experts who were teaching Soviet studies classes as the USSR was falling apart. You are always on safer ground when you understand that only God—all knowing and all powerful, if such a God even exists—could perhaps make the claim of being an expert. The rest of us are better off maintaining a large dose of doubt in our thinking. Realizing you know little or nothing is amazingly empowering. There is no question you won't be afraid to ask, out of concern that people will realize you aren't an "expert"—because you've never claimed to be one. Doubt is powerful.

Yet doubt is not an excuse for not thinking; it's not an excuse for ignorance. Doubt is an excuse to first get out and get the facts and then start a conversation—indeed, multiple conversations—as you begin to explore new ideas and theories. Today this is easy. The same technologies that now help hamper and even squash real conversation can ironically also provide the basis for real conversation. In the early days, we would use in-house database specialists to pull media reporting on keywords we'd give them to search. We thought it was really cutting-edge that our specialists also had access to foreign (non-U.S.) newspapers and magazines. That's how we'd read into a topic. That quickly changed when search engines arrived on the scene, and we could do the initial read-in on our desktops. Before there was Wikipedia, we had the CIA fact book online that allowed quickly accessible, reliable geopolitical information.

In our business today, managers, analysts, researchers, and even field operatives can quickly get a basic overview of the subject matter we are interested in. Often supplementing this with a few initial inquiries, we then put together an operational plan aimed at getting the information the client requires, effectively and discreetly. This is when it starts to get challenging. Topics span industries and locations around the globe. That's when we pull together the team and discuss how to proceed.

If the conversation were limited to the office, we would often get nowhere. The conference room just isn't always the best place for creative thinking.

Instead, we do some of our best brainstorming over a long lunch, good food and wine, good conversation. And then one of us says, "I was just thinking, maybe we come at that issue in Tanzania from a totally different angle. There was this banker I met when I was in Johannesburg last week. He mentioned having spent a few years in Dar es Salam and having good connections in the banking sector. Maybe he's our way in this time." And we talk through how the option of using the Johannesburg contact operating in Dar es Salam might play out. We look at the pros and the cons. The discussion is not personal. At issue isn't the person who made the suggestion, but the suggestion itself. Will it work or not?

There is something about talking about things outside of the office, in a comfortable setting. Big work problems all of a sudden take on a new perspective. This is especially so when it's put into the context of a larger conversation between friends that isn't focused on work.

Indeed, this goes not just for conversations with friends.

We try our best to run our business in this manner. With colleagues, we engage in open and nonjudgmental dialogue. That doesn't mean no criticism. The point is that the criticism is not about the person herself but about the work she did— where it fell short and how to make it better the next time.

With clients, we take the same view. You can be both professional and human at the same time. To be honest, we have it easy. Nearly all of our clients are involved in interesting things. We don't have to fake showing interest. When you show true interest, all the walls begin breaking down, and honest dialogue flows naturally.

When you put aside the aim of most talk—getting something out of the person you are speaking with—and instead focus on the person you are speaking about, the whole atmosphere begins to change. We're not talking about an idle exchange on how the family's doing before we "get down to business." That doesn't lead to real open conversation. It lacks the required honesty. You are asking about the family only as way in, perhaps to soften things a little before jumping into the business issues that need to be discussed. There is little sincerity in your question about the family. Your focus is on the goal. It shouldn't be, or at least it shouldn't completely be.

We had a Russian client several years ago who, if you just Googled his name, you might think was a descendant of a Russian version of Al Capone. The links mentioned allegations of organized crime connections, arms dealing, and even involvement in a murder. He was introduced to us by a mutual contact who came to us asking whether we could help. The contact explained that the Russian, now moderately well known in business and political circles—not just in the country but the world—felt he was getting a bad rap. The Russian wanted his name cleared, so an initial meeting was arranged in Moscow. We were taken from the airport by private car to an upscale restaurant not far from the Kremlin and shown to a private dining room on the second floor. The gentleman arrived soon after us. He told his security guard to wait outside. We exchanged pleasantries, and then he began to speak in Russian. Our mutual contact understood Russian and began translating, but we interrupted and asked whether the gentleman spoke English. He responded, "Not too well," but from our experience, lots (and lots) gets lost in translation. It is hard to really connect with someone when another person is interpreting, so we insisted that he speak in English as best he could, and he agreed. He began to speak and did not stop for nearly an hour. He told us his life story. Yes, in his younger years he had run in circles that in today's terms would be seen as criminal—but he had done nothing illegal. Russia in the late 1980s and early 1990s was a challenging place to operate, he explained (and we were well aware). He had opened up an import-export company in the early years of Perestroika and in that way made his first millions. And from there, his business expanded. He had contacts at high levels of the Russian government. "Is that a crime?" he asked rhetorically. We let him speak and then began asking him questions, taking detailed notes: names of contacts, businesses, business associates, government contacts in Russia, business and government contacts abroad—as many details as possible.

Then we explained to him: We could try to help, but first, he had to let us "check him out." In the private business intel, the term is *a self-due diligence*. We could only try to "clear his name" if we were convinced the allegations were indeed untrue.

He quickly agreed. We won't take you through all the steps we then followed, as they are not relevant to our discussion here, only to say that the guy checked out, and we were able to help him. What we want to emphasize, however, is the process, which was in many ways a conversation, even what we are describing here as a "real conversation." We had to be straight and truthful with our client, so he would be the same way with us. No, we can't promise you everything you want. There are things outside of our hands, we explained to him from the beginning. Reputation management in the age of the Internet is challenging, to say the least. And in his case, we explained to him that, no matter what, the going would be tough, given the difficult relations between Russia and many of the countries where the Russian businessman (who was now our client) felt he was being given a bad rap. Without digressing too much into the details, we live in a world where guilt is widely decided not on the basis of facts but on unfounded rumor. We can't control that. Nobody can. He understood what we were saying.

The point we are trying to make, though, is not about the work we did. It is about the manner in which it was done and relationships that can be built, even in business. We were able to help this client because we were straight with him, and we developed trust and understanding that allowed him to also open up to us. We listened. We didn't always agree, but we were always open. Certainly, there was much that we learned. We demonstrated sincere concern for him—not taking everything he said as gospel but listening and doing our best to set the record straight.

How did it go in the end? The guy, as we mentioned before, did check out. We were able to get that message across to several international law enforcement agencies that had him on their watch lists. But then, too, as we had anticipated might happen, he had enough contacts in high places in Moscow to make it difficult at the time we were involved to take the project where we had hoped. There were much bigger issues and players involved, and we could do little to prevent this guy from being swept away in the strong tides in which he found himself.

We prefer to be realistic and down to earth, but let's dream for a bit. Let's take this example of a Russian businessman basically being mistakenly categorized as a criminal in Western government and media circles, and consider what might have happened. A Russian businessman finds himself implicated in public debate over Russian-Western relations. He is initially accused of corruption and support for an allegedly corrupt Russian regime (in the eyes of some in the West). Facing these accusations, he not only denies them but says he is willing to answer any questions Western law enforcement or other government bodies may have about him and his activities. All he wants in return is to have his name cleared. In fact, what actually occurred is that Russian relations were at such a low point with the relevant Western nations that there was no chance for a successful dialogue to be initiated. He had already been classified as a "bad guy," and other nations showed no interest in having the classification changed, even if the facts showed otherwise. Now let's dream a little of a world in which people (and their leaders) are less eager to jump to conclusions that support their preconceived agendas and are willing to listen and, yes, also to learn. In such a world, a dialogue would have begun. The Russian businessman would have sat at a table with representatives of the Western nations, reviewed the issues, and tried to address any questions put to him. Where it should have been, the record would have been made straight. The Russian's name would have been cleared. But more important, as happens in these situations, a conversation would have begun. The Western officials and the Russian would have discussed current affairs, views of current political structures, and thoughts about the future. Both sides would have learned from the other. Both would have left the table enlightened and probably also ready for continued discussions.

There aren't, of course, always happy endings. Talking sometimes simply doesn't work. Yet it certainly increases the chances of success and, even if not complete success, at least it opens up lines of communications that can be helpful not just now but also in the future.

Real conversation is always good—in our personal lives, work, and society. Closing one's mind (and ears) to the Other in all realms of life is always a recipe for disaster.

We had another client, a Middle Eastern financier, who, as with the Russian case described previously, found himself the subject of a smear campaign. By "smear campaign," we mean a personal attack on his business and personal reputation carried out through the media and the Internet, as well as other means. In this case, the attackers had an easy target. It was easy for them to pull together a narrative that connected our client to terror financing and money laundering, even though there were no facts to support the allegations that quickly made their way into the media, law enforcement agencies, and government corridors. The methodology is simple, and there's no need to go into all of the details. It is enough to say that in a world now dominated by fake news, "guilt by association" is one of the simplest tactics to take when trying to make someone look bad. At its most basic level, it is the lowest form of profiling. In this case, you are Middle Eastern, Muslim, so you must also be a terrorist or, at minimum, a potential one. (Separately, we would note our late friend and advisory board member General Rashid Malek, a decorated Pakistani army officer, who had been sent for training to the United States in his younger years. He had close relations with many American, as well as other Western, officials and business people and complained bitterly about the treatment he received at U.S. airports simply on account of his name and appearance.) With wealthy commercial interests funding a smear campaign against him, the Middle Eastern financier tried largely unsuccessfully to push back. He was cut off from many financial markets and banks, due to obvious sensitivities about someone who faced money-laundering allegations, no matter how unsubstantiated. Guilt by association permeates bureaucracies and regulatory bodies as much as it does coffeehouse gossip. In a world where most people are happy dividing everything into simplistic dichotomies of good versus bad, it is easy to find yourself on the wrong side of the equation with really nothing to do to change things. Where there is no open, honest conversation, where the participants can't put aside preconceived notions and actually listen and try to learn and connect, you are left trapped. There is no way out.

Ironically, both sides are in effect trapped—both the attacker and the victim, so to speak. The victim is cornered, hemmed in by the allegations against her. The attacker is trapped by her own arguments—which, instead of being well thought out and open to change and refinement, are often nailed down in bias and old prejudices.

This closed-mindedness isn't merely bad, as a parent will tell a child who really doesn't understand why something is bad, but it simply is that way according to some arbitrary system of justice. It is bad because it is bad for the Other. It is bad because it is also bad for you. The outcome of a closed-minded approach will virtually always be inferior to that of an open-minded one, driven by dialogue and real conversation.

No, we don't live in a perfect world. We can't simply put our weapons down and believe that through talking we will solve all of our problems. That is naive and dangerous. But we can engage in more real conversations in our lives, businesses, and even politics, with the potential upside more than worth the potential risk. Real conversation opens up new avenues of thought and inquiry; it allows us to trust others in a responsible manner that can only bring good to all those involved.

This really goes to the heart of the argument. An attitude that has you open to the ideas, ideologies, feelings, and needs of those around you is ultimately good for you. It's not just good for the world. Being open minded and inquisitive and always willing to listen and learn, even from those who at first glance you would otherwise reject outright, is the best attitude to have for your own sake. This is not an appeal to some "head in the clouds," impractical way of living one's life. What we advocate here is something that isn't just the "right thing to do," but also the smart thing.

Real conversation is good for business. Again, it sounds counter-intuitive. It also, at face value, contradicts some of the characteristics we used to define real conversation—in particular, that at times one needs to enter a dialogue with no specific goal in mind. Business is by its very nature goal oriented. It would appear absurd to expect a business-related conversation not to be goal-driven. Now, there is nothing intrinsically wrong with being focused. In the business world, it is often seen as a plus. Yet there are also clear problems with this mode of engagement when you look at each of your actions, each of your conversations, according to how it will let you advance toward a specific goal or goals. It becomes easy to miss the proverbial forest when looking only at a few individual trees. You can undoubtedly end up setting the wrong goals or missing new potential avenues to address an issue or grow the business.

That is where honest conversation comes in. There is nothing more mind opening than letting your thoughts wander and truly listening and dropping preconceived notions. It is relaxing. It is invigorating. Your thinking becomes clearer. You begin to see what is really important. The excitement of this sudden lucidity is enrapturing. The power of the mind is opened, no longer reined in by petty personal agendas or even not-so-petty needs. Those can all wait. Set your mind free. Or, should we say, set your minds free—as our call is not to head off to a hidden cave in the mountains to meditate, but rather to reach greater awareness and self-awareness through true engagement with others, even in a business setting.

16

So Who's the Wise Guy?

> *Knowledge is knowing that a
> tomato is a fruit. Wisdom is not
> putting it in a fruit salad.*
> —Miles Kington

We have this everlasting debate about wisdom (we gave
you a taste of it in an earlier chapter)—whether there really is
such a thing, an amorphous state allegedly reached by certain
people in their lives where they have insight and knowledge
beyond the average person.

King Solomon is the classic example. Ecclesiastes, which
traditionally has King Solomon as the author, is one of the
centerpieces of the "wisdom books" of the Bible, with Proverbs
and Job, among others. These books allegedly provide wisdom:
insight into life obtained by a mysterious mix of experience,
knowledge, and the spiritual. One of Solomon's first acts as the
new king was to give judgment on a case involving two women
who each claimed the same baby as her own. In the classic tale,
Solomon orders the baby to be chopped in two, so the baby
can be divided equally between the two claimants. One of the

alleged mothers agrees. The other cries out that while she is indeed the real mother, she would rather see the child with the other woman than dead. Wisdom in this case allows Solomon to know—without actually checking the facts—who is the real mother. Do we actually know whether Solomon got it right? The reader is clearly meant to believe so. But maybe the mother who agreed to the baby being cut in two did so just to test the other alleged mother. Or maybe neither was the real mother. We will never know, of course. The message of the story isn't that a good judge must demand to see all the evidence, review it carefully, cross-exam the two sides, call witnesses, and so on. Rather, the message is that there is another path to making a correct decision, called "wisdom," with which King Solomon was blessed.

* * * * * *

We won't even touch on whether real conversation helps one become wiser (if wisdom even exists). But what we are emphatically saying is that it helps you get the answer correct.

Real conversation may or may not make you wiser, but it certainly makes you smarter, if *smarter* means capable of better understanding. You are presented with a problem. You can think about it yourself for a while, come up with some approaches to handling it, and perhaps do some online research to get additional insight. And then you can test it by presenting it to your colleagues—but not in the traditional manner, in which there are losers and winners around the conference table. Instead, through real conversation, there is honest and open discussion about the issue, and no opinion is dismissed out of hand. If the problem is a real tough one, leave it for a more formal discussion later or, better yet, an informal discussion outside the office. In the informal setting, there is more room for creativity and out-of-the-box thinking. The point is that there is no better state for figuring things out than by truly listening to, trusting, and engaging with another person. You may not end up wiser, but you certainly will be smarter, at least with regard to the specific issue at hand. Can you get more practical than that? Engage in real conversation because it will help you make better decisions.

Our three decades of conversations are a testament to that. Yes, the conversations have been at times fun and nearly always interesting and even enlightening. But they've also often been helpful—not only on a personal level, but also on a practical one. There is no shame in that.

There is more than a bit of irony in our position. We were having coffee with an old friend in New York City recently, at a prestigious Manhattan address with magnificent views of the city, including Central Park. We were talking about what a screwed-up world we live in, noting that no matter what your political views, the transition and change in the world's geopolitical climate, if not the real climate, are denied by no one. We live in a world in transition. As noted previously, our business is political and economic intel. The more difficult it is for government policy makers and business people to make decisions because they struggle to understand what is happening around them, the better it is for our business. People come to us to explain what is happening, to develop intelligence about topics normally related to business and political developments that in a more stable and transparent environment, they probably could get on their own or through simpler means. That's why, as wars broke out in the wake of 9/11 and then political and economic instability increased in the wake of the 2009 banking crisis, our business grew. For instance, clients called us in 2002 to figure out what the United States was going to do in Iraq and Afghanistan and how the situation might play out and affect domestic and international markets. In the years after the banking crisis, clients asked us to, for instance, help trace all their monies and debtors. Similarly, the friend with whom we were enjoying a coffee headed an investment house that specialized in making money in tough environments and knowing how to profit during good economic times, as well as bad. Instability for him meant opportunity, as it did for our firm. "Isn't it ironic," our friend said, "that we, of all people, want great stability, when it actually isn't good for our business models?" He went on to explain: "Look just here in America. Our firm is benefiting from Trump's policies, from everything from his lower taxes to the mess he is helping fuel in locations around the world. But I still don't like him and would like to see him out of office. But then the people who are really getting screwed by his policies, the working guy with the Make America Great Again cap, who still lives in an impoverished town in West Virginia or New York or Ohio, supports him. Where's the logic in it?" The logic is the same as that of the voters in towns across the UK who benefited big from being part of the EU (in the way of EU grants and other benefits) but still voted for Brexit. When the discussion is driven by emotion and not reason, you get unreasonable results. Even worse, when there is no longer conversation, when people aren't listening to anyone other than themselves and those who already agree with them, the results aren't going to be good.

Let's be clear. The problem is not the guys and the gals who voted for Trump and Brexit. Nor is it with those who voted against Trump and Brexit. The problem is the great divide between the camps. People seem to no longer see beyond their own tribe. We are becoming more and more divided. The divisions seem to be endless: your skin color, language, nationality, tribe, gender identity, sexual preference, heritage— the list just seems to keep growing. We have become experts at "standing up for ourselves," as individuals who demand to be seen and respected and as individuals who define themselves as a group because of their similarities. We go into defensive mode—rejecting ideas and people different from our own—in the name of sustaining our group. And then we are left with an ever-fracturing world, with each group looking out for its own and viewing outsiders only in relation to whether they do us good or bad. Our guard is up, and our minds are closed.

But it doesn't have to be that way. It should be obvious that people of different backgrounds don't have to be competing or clashing. The flip side of that statement may seem less obvious, but it is no less true: people of very different backgrounds, when brought together, not only don't need to be in conflict, they actually complement one another and can bring about fantastic results.

One recent evening, we had dinner with a few associates at a new trendy (that is, trendy for Cyprus) spot just inside Famagusta Gate. Sitting at the table was what might have appeared to be an odd group, although we'd prefer to describe it as *eclectic*. The roughly a dozen people included folks who had known one another for years and others who were meeting for the first time. Their nationalities ranged from American to English, Irish, Welsh, Maltese, Cypriot, South African, Ukrainian, and Pakistani. Religious and ethnic backgrounds were as varied. Ages went from twenty-five to eighty-plus-year-olds. The restaurant was in an old British colonial period building, the Venetian walls of Nicosia's Old City in full view from the large windows. A block down the narrow street, an old dilapidated barricade marked the border between the Greek section of the island and the northern section that had been occupied by Turkey since it invaded the country in 1974. Cypriot and Greek flags flew over the guard post nearby.

Certainly and admittedly from the perspective of most people in the world, we were "in the middle of nowhere," or certainly nowhere significant. The rich and famous, the movers and shakers, they are in cities like Paris or London or Beijing or Delhi, not in sleepy (and tiny) Nicosia. Around our table sat two former foreign ministers, two generals, and the former head of a national intelligence service. The scene was in many ways typical for sleepy Cyprus, which at least in recent decades has been a great meeting place for political, military, and intelligence officials from a wide variety of countries, sometimes even those in conflict with one another, who found the sleepy atmosphere a good location, at the vortex of more volatile areas of the Middle East, Central Asia, and Southern/Eastern Europe. In Cyprus, they could meet, often in secret but with a feeling of security they didn't have in their home countries. Most certainly, it was an atmosphere that allowed them to meet not just with friends, but also with enemies. Cyprus, in the last decades of the twentieth century and in many ways until this day, has permitted conversations to take place that could take place nowhere else.

Cyprus has been a divided island since the Turkish invasion in 1974, a no-man's land marked by barbed wire and abandoned buildings. Sporadic UN peacekeeping posts divide the country, including the capital, in two. An agreement in 2003 between Cyprus and Turkey allows residents (and tourists) some movement between the two parts of the country. But the division and the occupation remain real for residents of both sides. Both ethnic Turkish and Greek residents suffered and continue to feel the pain caused by the division—people were killed, homes were abandoned, livelihoods lost. Cyprus, at first glance, might be one of the last places one would look for a safe haven in which any kind of discussion between enemies could blossom. One might expect such an atmosphere to fuel hatred or at least unease, and not to provide a safe haven for discussion among sometimes the bitterest of enemies.

Our dinner gathering was not unique. A quiet island in the middle of nowhere (actually, quite strategically located in the eastern Mediterranean), Cyprus has over the years often been the host of numerous such seemingly odd-looking groups. There is no need to generalize or romanticize. Firsthand experience proves it: Odd is good. It is never boring and is often interesting. It is also often challenging and enlightening. You, of course, feel great warmth and comfort being around people similar to you, but what many people don't realize is that this special feeling of connection can also be reached with those who are different. Ideas and approaches and solutions, as well as all things connected to discourse and reasoning, are nourished when those sitting around the table are from different backgrounds and have different beliefs and attitudes. It does not take great wisdom to understand that decisions drawn from a group with strong and even conflicting views will largely be better than those made in a discussion by like-minded people. Opposites may or may not attract, but they most certainly can make for a great conversation.

17 *The Politics of Conversation*

All are banished till their conversations
appear more wise and modest to the world.
—William Shakespeare,
Henry IV, Part 2

WE ARGUE LIKE we really care. We've had friends angrily leave the table because they've been so fed up with our heated discussions about topics from religion and philosophy to science and culture and everything in between. We act like we care because we do care. The stakes are high. It is easy to forget it. It is even easier to simply discount talking as empty banter with no real importance. You don't have to be a know-it-all to have an opinion. You don't have to think your opinion must be the right one to want to start a dialogue. The opposite is the case. Conversation is about learning. It's about testing your ideas not in the safety of your own mind (indeed, how agreeable you can be when considering your own ideas), but in the muddy playing field of life. You may come out of the game a little bloodied, but you'll be all the better for it. And in this game, there are really no losers. Or then again, there are losers, big losers: those who don't participate.

Real conversation about issues that matter to individuals and societies reflects on the very essence of what it is to be human. So does real conversation as expressed not just in words but in the very encounter with the Other in genuine openness, empathy, and understanding. They are two sides of the same coin, providing the currency for which humanity can develop and improve. Without conversation, we are as good as dead. With conversation, the potential is endless. Humans grow, learn, connect, and discover through conversation. Conversation spans the material world and the spiritual world. It brings us art, just as it brings us science.

Conversation is radical. That is why it is so feared. Real conversation means everything is sacred and nothing is sacred. Respect, yes—but not to the point of giving up your ability to think and question. This is the dialogue championed by the likes of Buber and Freire. Buber, the Orthodox Jew, brave enough to put faith secondary to piety. Freire, the Brazilian educator, who dared to demand more than just bread for his country's oppressed but also real learning. Teach the masses to be freethinkers, and don't just focus on vocational training, he demanded. The military dictators ruling his country at the time immediately saw the threat. Any ruler with a totalitarian leaning would not think of kindly of young people educated to think critically.

It was an easy mistake to make in the immediate decades after World War II to believe that thinkers like Buber and Freire had prevailed. *Liberal* was a title to be proud of. It was less a reflection of a political position than an intellectual one. Liberal meant open-minded. It meant being free of petty ethnic and religious chauvinism. Equality and freedom became rallying cries literally around the world. Walls tumbled. Borders were opened. Technology appeared to further empower the liberal wave that swept the world. Those who didn't ride the wave were not just seen as pariahs, but also appeared to be really losing out, as greater freedom translated into greater wealth— or, at least, so it seemed. That is, until the bubble burst. The great liberal thinkers of the last century, such as Isaiah Berlin and Hannah Arendt, warned of human tendencies toward fascism but found their views drowned out by voices from Washington to Berlin and Beijing, who promised a new era of openness and opportunity. Their ideas were driven even deeper underground as the tech boom seemed to promise even greater opportunity and mobility. Fascism in the age of the Internet? The very idea seemed absurd. The World Wide Web seemed to be the harbinger of openness and freedom, an exchange of ideas, and possibilities for connections as endless as there are people with Internet service around the globe.

Yet the so-called experts got it wrong, as it seems they always do. Instead of greater openness and freedom, there were walls, and, even worse, Big Brother is now able to watch us virtually everywhere. Instead of closeness from more connections, the world became more divided and competitive. Conversation that should have flourished in this more open and fluid environment degenerated and appeared ready to die. The only dialogue permitted was between like-minded people. No one was interested any longer in hearing a different opinion, let alone in listening to a scathing criticism of his or her own views. That was now off limits. To attack someone's views became an attack on the person. The conversation became personal in the worst possible way.

How ironic that on the eve of the Internet boom, we had "We Are the World," "Hands across America," and "Live Aid," while in the immediate aftermath of the technology revolution, anything closely touching on political was banned from the annual Eurovision pop music competition.

The blame can be spread around. It would be as easy to place it on the political Right as it would be on the Left. Political parties worldwide from both camps have adopted small-minded outlooks that play to petty patriotism and ideologies, both religious and secular.

It's all fine and good for us to think conversation is important, but it will only really matter if others, as in lots of others, agree with us and try to make having real conversations an integral part of their lives. The reality of the situation is that today we are in the minority. Real conversation is a rarity. It is just not in style. It is despised in many quarters.

Why care? Because the death of conversation means the death of reason and rationality; it means the death of free thinking. This is no exaggeration. Just look at the world around us.

Few people are really talking to one another anymore. People continue to give orders. They continue to instruct and direct, to demand and plead, to argue, to shout and scream. We explored in an earlier chapter how technology has intensified the noise. Lots of shouting and screaming happens on the Internet. There is little connection. People hold tight to their beliefs. They fear people and ideas different from their own. They stick with their own. Ours is a world of Us versus Them. There are bridges between the two, but they are few and narrow. Just ask a Syrian refugee refused entry into Europe. The Other is too often seen as a threat. Our world is one in which immigrants have made countless contributions to their new homes, but somehow *immigrant* has become a dirty word for many. New and different, instead of offering exciting possibilities, are seen as threats. The Other is rejected outright, categorized as dangerous, and told that she is not wanted and should go home.

Let's be clear: The rejection of Others, the denial of conversation, is not just wrong. It will also lead to disaster and, indeed, has already led there in many instances. This is not to say that, for instance, there is only one acceptable policy on immigration that allows refugees unrestricted access to the country of their choosing. Or to say that there is something intrinsically wrong with patriotism and ethnic binds. Rather, it is to say that policies based on arbitrary criteria born in ignorance are doomed to failure. When there is no true dialogue, when there is no true conversation, when leaders and their supporters are doing all the talking but not listening, they get what they deserve: disaster.

Closing the door to real conversation is closing the door to reason and knowledge. All thinking creatures can begin a dialogue in their minds and then expand outward to friends, families, colleagues, and acquaintances; this has been the engine for the evolution of humanity. The dialogue can and does include emotion and spirit. We aren't robots. Thinking is freedom, not destiny. If we allow ourselves to think freely, we can create our own destiny. But if we refuse to really listen and talk, if we cling to beliefs only because they are dictated by our community or tradition, we suffocate. We won't be the only victim; so will our world.

Leaders who preach for division and separation have a great appeal. There is a sense of safety in divisions, in walls that keep the feared "Others" on the outside and those on the inside oppressed. Granted, there are times when a true enemy or criminal must be kept at bay, but those are the exceptions. There is an inherent contradiction in advocating greater division for the sake of security and development. Walls limit. More walls create greater limitations. A world in which ethnic, religious, and political groups look to the other in fear and advocate divisions to keep them all separated is a world oppressed. No one is safe. On both sides of the fence, the people are ultimately living in fear.

If the end of conversation meant silence, we would be lucky. There can be peace in silence. What we have today as conversation disappears is the opposite of peace and quiet. Just listen . . . Can you bear the screaming and shouting any more? The world seems to be divided between those who have joined the fight, and those who just can't take it anymore and instead have turned the channel: no more news, no more talk shows, no more politically and ideologically driven Facebook feeds. But there is nowhere to hide. If you join the fray, you get crushed in the battle. If you try to flee, you still are likely to get hit by the shrapnel.

There is no fleeing. You must choose.

You already know where we stand on the topic. Conversation has done very well by us. It is from our personal experience that we have become believers in the power of conversation, real conversation, and at this juncture we say real *political* conversation. It shouldn't be a dirty word, *political*. In its broadest of meanings, *political* encompasses all of our relations with others that go beyond the purely personal. It covers all of our interactions with our communities, countries, and world. Real conversation is at its very essence political. It

reflects concern for the world. It is as grand as that sounds—
"reflecting concern for the world"—but also down to earth
in understanding the need for a practical application for all
of those grand ideas. Caring means truly caring and not just
paying lip service. Just saying you care is not enough. You must
really care. And differentiating between those pretending to be
concerned and really being concerned actually isn't difficult.
The fakes eventually are uncovered. Sincerity shines forth. Lies
bring darkness.

We've seen in our own lives what opening up and engaging
with others in an honest, nonjudgmental, and, perhaps most
important, undemanding way can do. Our personal lives have
benefited. Our work has benefited.

Our world has benefited? We won't even touch the
question. We aren't so arrogant as to believe we have actually
done anything big with our lives. But as we have explored our
communities and our world, we also have no doubt that it isn't
always just the so-called big things that matter. Indeed, the big
things can appear overwhelming. It is easy to throw up your
hands and just say, "I give up." This is particularly so in the face
of the daunting challenges of our day. Over half a century ago,
Bertrand Russell warned BBC radio listeners about what he
saw as a growing tendency toward listlessness and fatalism that
was disastrous to vigorous life.

"I constantly receive letters that say, 'I see that the world
is in a bad state, but what can one humble person do? Life and
property are at the mercy of a few individuals who have the
decision over peace or war. Economic activities on a large scale
are determined by those who govern either the state or the
large corporations. Even where there is nominal democracy, the
part that one citizen can play in controlling policy is usually

infinitesimal. Is it not perhaps better in such circumstances to forget public affairs and get as much enjoyment by the way as the times permit?' I find such letters difficult to answer, and I am sure that the state of mind that leads to their being written is very inimical to a healthy social life.[39]"

Each of us certainly matters to ourselves and our families, colleagues, friends, and communities. We matter in that our actions and behavior clearly have an influence on our immediate surroundings, just as we are influenced by those in our immediate surroundings. There are, of course, those with more wealth and power. The titans of industry and politics may in many areas be the ones calling the shots, but let's not give them too much credit. Let's also not underestimate the role and influence of the masses.

It isn't easy, and we certainly are far from perfect. Or how about we are very imperfect, just like everyone else? Maybe even a little worse. We don't live ideal lives. Like everyone, we often use others—engaging with people having our own personal gain in mind. We normally ignore those around us for the most part, and when we really look at them, it is as a means to an end.

There are those who tell us that simply is "the way it is." We, however, prefer the American pop singer Nick Hornsby's take on that line: "Don't you believe them."

Standing in line, marking time
Waiting for the welfare dime
'Cause they can't buy a job
The man in the silk suit hurries by

---

[39] Bertrand Russell, *Authority and the Individual* (the first of the Reith Lectures) (London: George Allen & Unwin, 1949), pp. 36–37.

As he catches the poor old lady's eyes
Just for fun, he says, "Get a job."
That's just the way it is
Some things will never change
That's just the way it is
Ah, but don't you believe them
Said hey, little boy, you can't go where the others go
'Cause you don't look like they do
Said hey, old man, how can you stand to think that way?
Did you really think about it before you made the rules?
He said, Son
That's just the way it is
Some things will never change
That's just the way it is
Ah, but don't you believe them.[40]

Things are often terrible. Slavery, genocides, wars, family violence, rape—all since time began. All still with us, maybe even worse these days in many areas, although we'd like to think otherwise.

And then there are those magical moments. Mahatma Gandhi, thin-bodied with round eyeglasses and wearing a simple loincloth, standing up against an empire. Martin Luther King Jr. declaring, "I had a dream," on the Lincoln Memorial stairs, in an environment of Jim Crow laws and open racial prejudices, still holding on to a vision that "little black boys and black girls will be able to join hands with little white boys and white girls as sisters and brothers."

---

[40] "The Way It Is" lyrics © Zappo Music, Sony Atv Music Publishing France.

And things did change. It was never easy and the change never complete, and often the struggle continues. Yet this is not the same world as a century ago or a millennium ago or even a decade ago, in many ways. Yes, things have gotten better.

The Hornsby song cautions, "It only goes so far." Life is not easy, and that makes it easy—or, at least, easier—to go about our daily lives just trying to survive. This allows us to largely ignore the implications of our actions on those around us.

We act in this matter ignorant of the fact that this behavior is ultimately bad for us, too. Or maybe we're not so ignorant. We are trying to survive, correct? That means we can do whatever is needed. Screw our neighbors if it comes to that; certainly ignore the needs of other societies. Enemies—that's an easy one: annihilate them if necessary, even if it includes the innocent among them. Future generations aren't even a consideration when the question is boiled down to survival today.

We think we are getting ahead. Yes, some others are paying the price, we tell ourselves, but this is just the way it is and always will be. But is it? And are we in fact actually not getting "ahead" but, on the contrary, getting lost?

"If I am not for myself, then who will be for me? But when I am for myself, then what am I?"[41] Now go figure that one out. Sounds easy. Read it again: "If I am not for myself, then who will be for me? But when I am for myself, then what am I?" Isn't the Jewish sage Hillel, who wrote this, trying to have it both ways? Yes, he's saying, it's okay to look out for yourself. But if you only look out for yourself, then it's not okay.

---

[41] Hillel, *Sayings of the Fathers*, 1:14.

Where to draw the line? When to say yes to asylum seekers and when, no; what is the best model for assisting a country's poor; how much to budget to allocate for defense. . . . These aren't easy questions. Today, the political Left in Europe has lost much of its credibility for failing to show even a willingness to understand, as Hillel did a century before Jesus was born, that there is an important balancing act that must be maintained that allows us to look out for ourselves without ignoring the needs of others. And many on the political Right look like arrogant and stupid fools for their callous treatment of immigrants so badly in need of help. Maybe Hillel would be laughing at us. Like all good Jewish sages, he gives us answers that aren't really answers but rather openings of other questions. The conversation continues. It will continue for eternity, for there is no Answer. The conversation is eternal. There are streams of Orthodox Judaism that certainly argue otherwise. They claim to hold the Answers. But as with other orthodoxies, they crumble under the weight of free thinking, no matter how much they try to squash it.

Or maybe Hillel would be crying. Reason, for all that it has given to humankind, still plays second fiddle to our whims and passions. Just ask David Cameron. Or Vladimir Putin, Donald Trump, Mateusz Morawiecki, Recep Tayyip Erdogan, or any of the long list of leaders who in the first decades of the new millennium have come to and remained in power based on populist agendas. Don't fall into the trap of the Left and equate populism with ignorance or evil. That just doesn't play to what these populist leaders are spreading with their demagoguery. It is also elitist, unfair, and simply wrong. Populism exists equally on both the Left and the Right. And Reason is equally missing on both sides.

Just try to have a political discussion that doesn't blow up into an exchange of accusations largely personal. There is little discussion of the actual issues. "My reason is not obliged to bow and bend; my knees are."[42] Think about it. This shouldn't just be an empty slogan. We go through our lives largely being told what to do. Even worse, we are told what to think. We are told what is right or wrong. At one time, and for many this still applies, rabbis or priests or imams and the like were the holders of Truth. Then philosophers; today scientists—not to mention political leaders.

The twenty-first century has not only brought us talk of an era of post-truth and completely blurred the lines between true and false with allegations that just about everything is fake news. The new millennium also has given us the *narrative*. It is no longer a term that we in the over-fifty generation knew simply as the story line of a book or another work of fiction or even nonfiction. Instead, narrative has become the story line of all things political—the way a particular individual or members of a group view their story and wants others to also view it. You see where this is going and indeed has already gone: the story takes on the primary role; facts become secondary at best.

Politicians have become experts at manipulating our post-truth, narrative-preoccupied world. Among the most fashionable narratives: The ones that reflect a twenty-first-century version of patriotism not based on ideals, but rather a portrayal of the nation's future as being at great risk, which demands that its immediate needs must be met at all costs, even if it means completely ignoring and even trampling on the needs

---

[42] Michel de Montaigne, *Essays: On Conversation,* (*London, Penguin Books,* 2004).

of others (from potential immigrants to long-standing allies). This is patriotism at its lowest common denominator. The goal is survival of the "nation at threat." All ideals are thrown out the window—and, in many cases, also any semblance of morality. Then there are the narratives that can be seen as taking "patriotism" to another extreme, whereby every group presents itself as unique and not only indivisible, but also incapable of having its "uniqueness" threatened. Black American football players take their knees during the playing of their country's national anthem; professors at American universities must "warn" students if an upcoming lecture might offend their sensitivities, both personal and political. It is as if criticism has become a dirty word. There is no room for debate, no room for having your ideas critiqued and challenged. "Feelings" are given priority over reason. They are given a virtually holy status: it is forbidden to trample in any way on the sanctity of someone's feelings. In the name of creating a "safe space," debate is quashed. Individuals—whether the guy or the gal on the street or the politician sitting in Parliament—are left secure in their beliefs and ideologies, with critics put on the defensive, unable to challenge an opposing position not for lack of strong arguments, but due to debate being de facto forbidden.

There is no conversation. No discussion. No debate. No exchange of ideas and theories. No interaction that might even bring new and better ideas and strategies. Everyone is afraid of hurting someone's feelings. If people speak about the topic at all, it is with hesitation and even fear that they will be accused of being insensitive or, worse, a racist or a chauvinist or whatever the latest trend may dictate. The line has disappeared between "I disagree with you" and "I dislike you." It is all personal now: it is about the person, not about the idea.

Everything is viewed in the light of the narrative (of whichever your choosing). Forget about debating the actual issues, looking at the facts, or attempting an analysis. Instead, the focus is on the narrative that each side holds to, as if it were delivered to them and only to them at Mt. Sinai.

This leaves us with a world where we are being told what is right or wrong, what is the truth, and what we must hold to. At the same time, we are rarely told how to try to figure out what the truth is ourselves.

The sixteenth-century French essayist Michel de Montaigne, who challenged us to use our reason and not let it bend, recognized at least in part what humankind was up against. "That which I myself adore in Kings is the crowd of adorers; all reverence and submission are due to them," Montaigne writes, "except that of understanding."[43]

Montaigne, writing under French monarch rule, had to be careful with his words. Today, at least in some parts of the world, we can put in more bluntly: "Screw you, king; screw you, priest or rabbi or imam. Who put you in charge of what I'm supposed to think?"

Yet even today we need to guard our words. In many parts of the world, attacking the political or the religious can still land you in jail. And more subtle forms of "thought control" exist in those places that claim to be the most free—just ask an American university professor who must be careful not to "offend" students.

The fact that five centuries since Montaigne's call for free thinking and reason these far from prevail should really make us worry.

---

[43] Ibid.

We aren't encouraged to think for ourselves, and we aren't taught to think for ourselves. That's how bad things are and will continue to be. We need to know that it is all right to think for ourselves, to come to our own opinions, to figure things out on our own, and, most important, to look at things critically. "Critically" doesn't mean in a negative light. Instead, "critically" means using our own independent reason in order to gain understanding and not simply accepting what we are told, no matter who is telling us.

Question others, in order to truly understand. Here is where conversation comes in, for conversation is the ultimate tool of the mind. Come up with your own ideas; explore them in your own mind, or perhaps read something online or from a library to start exploring the significance of what you've come up with. And then start putting it to the test of a good conversation.

A conversation is the best place to have your own ideas and beliefs tested. It's never easy, but if you're sharing ideas with someone close to you, it can often be painless. Accept the challenge. Don't look for reinforcement, speaking only to people who will agree with you. Speak to those who have opposing views or are independent-minded.

"So contradictory judgments neither offend or irritate me; they merely wake me up and provide me with exercise. We avoid being correct: we ought to come forward and accept it, especially when it comes from conversation."[44]

The current rage is to say that many of our problems today arise from the fact that we are talking to and, in many cases, just listening to (and reading) those with whom we

---

[44] Ibid.

already agree. In the United States, this is broadly described as the viewers of Fox News versus viewers of CNN. Trump supporters/Republicans with Fox. Democrats with CNN. So the CNN attacks on Trump are being heard (and talked about) only by folks who already don't like the president. And the same with Fox News: the station's support of Republicans over Democrats and of Trump, in particular, is being heard only by Republicans who already support him.

This view is at best simplistic. For the purposes of our discussion, this view should not be presented as something new. Particularly outside the United States, in most democratic countries media outlets are known to be broken down into those that support a particular party or agenda and those that are more independent leaning. People hanging out with people who are like themselves is nothing new, so it's too easy to say that this is the cause of all of our ills.

Yes, there is great irony in the fact that in recent years such political entrenchment and division have occurred in a country that prided itself on being a so-called melting pot of ethnic and religious groups. But that is simply because it was mistakenly assumed that the melting pot brought everyone together. In fact, it simply cooked up a stew of different groupings, so, for instance, unemployed white and immigrant families in the U.S. rust belt could all be fed up with what they see as the Democratic Party failing them. Groups remain; they are simply different than they were a decade or two ago.

What is more troubling is the lack of true dialogue, both on a political and a personal level. By dialogue, we mean real open conversations with others and even better if they are from a different group or background than you.

Our current condition isn't just bad for the world, it's also bad for us. In ignoring those around us, we ultimately are also ignoring ourselves.

It is largely only at certain junctures in our lives when reality hits us with a bombshell, such as when a friend or a family member passes away or something simply horrific has occurred somewhere in the world that catches our attention. Then we suddenly open our eyes to all that we have missed by focusing only on ourselves. For that brief moment, we shed tears over what we haven't pad attention to. We, of course, are really crying for ourselves, for our loss, for our pathetically wasted lives that we spent running after things that don't actually matter at all.

We have ignored others. We have misused others. And we have, at the same time, ignored our true selves.

Yes, we must work hard. We must protect ourselves and our families and communities. Life is not easy. But the fact that life is difficult doesn't give us a free pass to be completely self-centered.

Or does it?

This is the point that Montaigne missed. He recognized the State and the Church as threats. Other traditional forms of political and cultural power structures that are similarly a threat to free thinking also come to mind when we read Montaigne, including even threats within a community or a family.

But what about human nature?

History is filled with the blood of our fellow humans killed in the name of the survival of Us at the expense of the Other. The terminology changes. The Other is the barbarian, the foreigner, the immigrant, the alien, the gentile, the Jew, or the person of color. The names we call those who are unlike us are many. These are the others we are taught to fear and despise. They, we are told, are ruining our neighborhood, raping our wives, destroying our culture. They cause all of our ills.

The Other becomes the scapegoat. By putting all that is "bad" on others, we leave all the "good" to ourselves. They are the destroyers of culture, and we are the cultured. They are rapists, and we, the gentlemen. They are the primitive, and we, the sophisticated.

We are left talking to ourselves.

We could argue all day (and all night if the company were good enough) about human nature and where it will lead us (of course, if there is such as thing as human nature, and who knows anyway what will come tomorrow, especially in our screwed-up world?). But it seems clear that in a world where we aren't really talking, and when we are talking it's just with like-minded people, our chances aren't too good.

That's what we are left with when we close ourselves off from others who are different from us. We are just left with ourselves, homogeneous and boring—and often dangerous in our unfounded, primitive fears of those who aren't like us.

How stupid we are indeed. We have ignored and forgotten the lessons of history, both modern and ancient.

Tragically, there is no lack of leaders, whether political, religious, or even business, who largely for their own interests and their own gain fuel the hatred of Others. That marks the beginning of the end of real conversation. When the Other is not only not listened to, but considered the enemy, there can be no conversation. And it all starts to crumble, all the good that men and women of reason and creativity have done, all of their free thinking that has brought humankind to great heights in the arts and sciences, in philosophy and mathematics, and, yes, even in politics and society. It all begins to crumble when real conversation stops.

It's up to us.

"In a place where there are no men, strive to be a man."[45]

"And if not now, when?"[46]

So go to it. Start a conversation before it's too late.

---

[45] Hillel, *Sayings of the Fathers*, 2:4.

[46] Ibid., 1:14.

Afterword

$\mathcal{T}$HE BRITISH MATHEMATICIAN Alfred North Whitehead wrote that "the philosophical tradition consists of a series of footnotes to Plato." Realizing that goes for most unscientific matters in nature, we jumped reluctantly into writing this book. Did we really have anything new to add? We still don't know. Let the reader be the judge.

We were somewhat encouraged when early on in the writing process, we did a quick Wikipedia check and discovered all it had to say about conversation at the time was that it was "interactive communication between two or more people" and that "conversation skills" are an "important part of socialization."

We aren't knocking Wikipedia; we use it all the time, including in our work. What encouraged us, when we asked ourselves whether conversation was a topic worthy of addressing or was already over-addressed, was that it appeared the latter was the case. Sadly, as we had guessed, conversation just wasn't a sexy topic. At best, it was taken for granted. At worst, it was simply on the way out: who needs real face-to-face conversation in the age of the smartphone?

Another concern of ours: maybe we were just two guys who liked to drink and enjoyed the bullshitting that comes with it. Here again, however, we were saved. In doing some initial research on our topic, we ran into Montaigne's essay on conversation, which we quoted extensively. But what made us instant friends of this sixteenth-century essayist (actually, the inventor of the essay) was this comment:

"Has anyone ever acquired intelligence through logic? Where are her beautiful promises? 'Nec ad melius vivendum nec ad commodius disserendum' (I would prefer a son of mine to learn the talk of the tavern, rather than of our university yap-shops)."[47]

Now, there is a man after our hearts. So off we went, writing. We really had no idea where we were headed. We've admitted earlier that we had to ditch our initial plan of taping a series of our conversations and then editing them down for a book. We quickly learned that conversation isn't easily translated into text. This is particularly so in our instance, when we hadn't set out to write conversation in a play or for theater. Of course, that isn't conversation at all, but rather dialogue, perhaps a first cousin of conversation but certainly not the real thing.

We dropped the idea of compiling a book of our conversations and instead decided to focus on what conversation had meant for us. We just knew that conversation, our conversation as friends for the last thirty years and the conversations we have had with others, had been an important

---

[47] *In dialectica autem vestra nullam existimavit esse nec ad melius vivendum nec ad commodius disserendum vim. In physicis plurimum posuit.* (Logic, on which your school lays such stress, [Epicurus] held to be of no effect either as a guide to conduct or as an agent to thought. Natural Philosophy he deemed all-important.)—Cicero, *De Finibus Bonorum et Malorum*, Book I, Line 63.

part of our lives. We wanted to share this experience with others.

Part of the experience of real conversation is that of stepping back. A disengagement takes place on one level of our lives—the level where we busy ourselves with the sometimes challenging and difficult, oftentimes boring and mundane, and, if we are lucky, at times beautiful and enlightening rigors of living. It is indeed often tough. So tough that we, for the most part, turn our brains on autopilot for most of the day. There is too much going on to actually think—until we pause, step back, and put aside for a bit the demands of our lives. But then don't disappear, either into your own mind or, like ancient hermits, to some remote mountain or desert retreat. Instead, reconnect with the world by connecting with an Other or Others, who have also taken a step back.

So we talk. We think and we talk more. We explore what we believe and experience and hold to be true for ourselves and our world. We do this openly and honestly. We don't fear rejection or isolation. We talk without judging or concern that we will be judged. We bravely leave everything open to questioning. There are no sacred cows.

As much as the writing of this book has parallels to our actual conversations, certainly one common element is that we had no idea where the process would take us. The reader will ultimately be the judge whether we took the correct course or got badly lost.

We certainly did not set out to write a political book. Our aim at the outset was not to write a treatise about the importance of free thinking and how the human tendency toward fascist resolutions to the complex challenges of political life seems to be our destiny, unless we fight with all of our might against it. The goal was not to demonstrate how the lack of real human engagement through open and free dialogue reflects our world's larger political and social woes. And most certainly, we did not set out to be crusaders armed with weapons forged in a crucible of conversation and leading the fight against closed-mindedness and its tyranny. It, of course, didn't "just turn out that way." If you were the bartender or the waitress at one of our favorite watering holes who over the years caught a little bit of what we were always arguing about, you probably could have guessed. The longing to understand ourselves and the world, to make the world a better place (but admittedly doing more talking about it than actually helping), is what has driven our decades-long conversation.

There is certainly a danger in writing about "our conversation of more than thirty years," of thinking about it, and sitting in front of a computer and recording what we think about our conversation and the importance of conversation in general. The danger is that what should be a completely relaxed, unselfconscious affair all of sudden becomes something we aren't just doing naturally but are now thinking about. It sounds a little odd. Yes, on one hand, "thinking" and "conversing" are intimately linked. That is one of the messages of this book—the power of talking through ideas, not just thinking about them. Scientists, especially mathematicians and physicists, often refer to a "thought experiment": setting out and testing ideas in your own mind. That, of course, is an important methodology. Yet the real work starts when you test that hypothesis in the minds of others, when you allow your ideas to be questioned and debated and criticized. On the other hand, real conversation ultimately isn't about simply testing ideas and hypotheses. It is about connecting with others. It is about talking openly and honestly. It is letting your thoughts flow, which doesn't go well with being self-conscious.

If this book can make only a tiny dent in increasing people's awareness of the importance of real engagement with those around us—friends and families, but also strangers and even "enemies"—it was worth the effort. The book has indeed become a call to arms. You must speak—and listen. You must care what your worst enemy thinks. You must be willing to defend rationally all you believe, care for, and hold true and reject those who encourage you to sit smugly entrapped with ideas and beliefs that you have never really put to the test. We don't live in a perfect world and never will. (And maybe we are lucky this is so.) Listening and talking won't solve everything. And while in the short term conversation is always the best option, in some instances there may indeed be no more to say (at least, for the moment). But overall, there is no other way for us to proceed, as individuals, societies, and the world as a whole: we must embrace conversation, real conversation, or we are doomed.

Don't be mistaken. Don't make the mistake that those who are in power or strive for power always make, of thinking they are strong enough to impose their will, so there is no need for dialogue, no need for free and open discourse because they already know all the facts. Embrace others, especially those who are different and think differently from you.

We began our conversation after a long night in a tense, crowded, loud newsroom: a forty-something Irish RAF nuclear-bomber pilot turned journalist, and a Jewish-American wannabe reporter just out of university. Not much in common. Certainly very different opinions and beliefs. But that only made the conversation that much more interesting.

We had no expectations about the conversation then, no plan for how it would go or where it would take us, if anywhere. In some ways, the writing of this book was similar. We didn't know where it would lead.

So, get out there. Be brave. Don't be afraid. Put your phone aside, even if just for a bit. Look that other person in the eyes, look deeply into his or her eyes, . . . and get talking. Start a conversation. And we, of course, mean really talking, with care and empathy, an open mind and heart. The beer in hand is optional.

About the Authors

Thomas O'Dwyer, born in Tipperary, Ireland, is a former RAF aircrew officer who later became an international journalist. He had more than twenty years of Middle East experience as a writer and an editor with Reuters and other foreign and regional media in Cyprus, Bahrain, Lebanon, and Israel. He rote personal columns in the *Jerusalem Post*, the *International Herald Tribune* and the *Encyclopedia Britannica Yearbook*. He has written for the *Guardian* and *openDemocracy* magazine and broadcast for the BBC and RTE Irish radio. He has a personal column in 3 *Quarks Daily* online magazine.

Bill Hutman, born in Washington, D.C., has worked in the private intelligence field for over twenty years, managing companies based in Washington, D.C.; London; and Nicosia. Previously, Bill spent a dozen years as an investigative reporter and writer, and his work has appeared in the *New York Times* and the *Times of London*, as well as publications by Harvard University Press and Syracuse University Press. Bill has a bachelor's degree from the University of Virginia and a master's degree from the School of Advanced International Studies, Johns Hopkins University.

www.ingramcontent.com/pod-product-compliance
Lightning Source LLC
Chambersburg PA
CBHW032348280326
41935CB00008B/492